THE MOST LOW-DOWN, LOUSIEST, LOATHSOME THINGS EVER SAID

ALSO BY STEVEN D. PRICE

Teaching Riding at Summer Camp

Panorama of American Horses

Civil Rights (volumes 1 and 2)

Get a Horse: Basics of Back-Yard Horsekeeping

Take Me Home: The Rise of Country & Western Music

The Second-Time Single Man's Survival Handbook (with William J. Gordon)

Old as the Hills: The Story of Bluegrass Music

Horseback Vacation Guide

Schooling to Show: Basics of Hunter-Jumper Training (with Anthony D'Ambrosio Jr.)

The Whole Horse Catalog

The Complete Book of Horse & Saddle Equipment (with Elwyn Hartley Edwards)

Riding's a Joy (with Joy Slater)

All the King's Horses: The Story of the Budweiser Clydesdales

The Beautiful Baby-Naming Book

Riding for a Fall

The Polo Primer (with Charles Kauffman)

The Ultimate Fishing Guide

Caught Me a Big'Un (with Jimmy Houston)

The American Quarter Horse

Two Bits' Book of the American Quarter Horse

The Quotable Horse Lover

Essential Riding

The Horseman's Illustrated Dictionary

The Greatest Horse Stories Ever Told

Classic Horse Stories

1001 Smartest Things Ever Said

1001 Dumbest Things Ever Said

1001 Insults, Put-Downs, and Comebacks

The Best Advice Ever Given

1001 Funniest Things Ever Said

1001 Best Things Ever Said About Horses

1001 Greatest Things Ever Said About California

The Quotable Billionaire

What to Do When a Loved One Dies (reissued as More Than Sympathy)

The World's Funniest Lawyer Jokes

Endangered Phrases

Excuses for All Occasions

The Little Black Book of Writers' Wisdom

Gut Busters and Belly Laughs

How to Survive Retirement

The Most Inspiring Things Ever Said

THE MOST LOW-DOWN,

Lousiest,

Loathsome

THINGS EVER SAID

Edited and with an Introduction by

STEVEN D. PRICE

Guilford, Connecticut

An imprint of Globe Pequot

Distributed by NATIONAL BOOK NETWORK

British Library Cataloguing-in-Publication Information available

Library of Congress Cataloging-in-Publication Data available

ISBN 978-1-4930-2944-0 (paperback)
ISBN 978-1-4930-2945-7 (e-book)

♾™ The paper used in this publication meets the minimum requirements of American National Standard for Information Sciences—Permanence of Paper for Printed Library Materials, ANSI/NISO Z39.48-1992.

CONTENTS

• • • • • •

XVII

INTRODUCTION

. . . .

Mass communication has taken great strides since the advent of radio and television, and even greater ones since social media invaded the Internet. However, whether "great" in this context means "wonderful" or merely "big" depends on your perspective. Although we can now learn about, and even witness, events happening all over the world even as they're happening, we can also be subjected to all manner of false information or plain drivel . . .

. . . And to low-down, lousy, and loathsome remarks. Whether that's great depends on who's going the remarking end and who's on the receiving end.

When Andy Warhol predicted that everyone would have his or her fifteen minutes of fame, he never dreamed that the time it takes to post something on Twitter, Facebook, or other social media was all the time that achieving notoriety would take. Or the time it takes for a "reality" television show appearance, or a phone call to a shock-jock radio program. And the more outrageous a shocking or abusive utterance is, the faster and more widely circulated it becomes.

Yes, this is indeed the Age of Acrimony. Not that hurling or writing insults began with the cathode ray tube or the silicon chip, but the ready availability to calling attention to oneself proliferated with instruments of mass communication. Add to that the ebbing of societal condemnation of what many still regard as foul language, and the result is more venom that a cage full of cobras.

These pages contain what I hope are the best of bad-mouth.

Lest anyone think that the 2016 presidential campaign was the low-water mark of political vituperation, take a look at what our Founding Fathers had to say about each other. For example, Alexander Hamilton's judgment of Thomas Jefferson: "The moral character of Jefferson was repulsive. Continually puling about liberty, equality and the degrading curse of slavery, he brought his own children to the hammer, and money of his debaucheries." (Hardly the lyrics of a Broadway musical).

Witty insults take various forms, such as Dorothy Parker's assessment of Katharine Hepburn's acting ability: "She runs the gamut of emotions from A to B"; and Mae West's "His mother should have thrown him away and kept the stork." British political figures have been particularly adept in this department. Prime Minister Benjamin Disraeli explained the difference between a misfortune and a calamity this way: "If [rival William] Gladstone fell into the Thames, that would be a misfortune; and if anybody pulled him out, that would be a calamity."

Movie reviewers are adept at letting loose with both barrels: "Only—repeat only—for those who thought *Police Academy 5* was robbed at Oscar time," said Leonard Maltin about *Police Academy 6*; "On the IMDB trivia page it says 'The most amazing thing about *Pirates 3* is that they started filming without a completed script.' No, they finished filming without a completed script," was Mark Kermode's take on *Pirates of the Caribbean: At World's End*.

The English-speaking world doesn't have a lock on insults. The French say,

"You are as smart as the bottom of your feet;" the Italians, "Take a dump in your hand and then slap yourself;" and in Yiddish (a language rich in curses) is the wish that "I should outlive him long enough to bury him."

Okay, you get the idea.

After mucking about the insults and curses cesspool for these many months, I selected my favorites, which you'll find in the concluding "Editor's Choices" chapter.

All right, you want low-down? There are insults and curses that are so wince-some you'll recoil. Lousy? There are insults so lousy that even lice would think twice about using them. And loathsome? Don't even ask. Read, laugh, or wince, remember them, and—at your own risk—sprinkle liberally or conservatively into your conversations.

—Steven D. Price

Chapter

· · · · · · · · · · · ·

I

Presidential Poison:
Blackening the White House

If ever a nation was debauched by a man, the American nation has
been debauched by [him]. If ever a nation was deceived by
a man, the American nation was deceived by [him].
—THE *PHILADELPHIA AURORA* ON GEORGE WASHINGTON

. . . and as to you, sir, treacherous in private friendship . . . and a
hypocrite in public life, the world will be puzzled to decide
whether you are an apostate or an imposter, whether you have
abandoned good principles, or whether you ever had?
—THOMAS PAINE TO GEORGE WASHINGTON

That dark designing sordid ambitious vain proud arrogant and
vindictive knave.
—GENERAL CHARLES LEE ON GEORGE WASHINGTON

It has been the political career of this man to begin with hypocrisy,
proceed with arrogance, and finish with contempt.
—THOMAS PAINE ON JOHN ADAMS

He is vain, irritable, and a bad calculator of the force and probable
effect of the motives which govern men.
—THOMAS JEFFERSON ON JOHN ADAMS

. . . hideous hermaphroditical character, which has neither the force
and firmness of a man, nor the gentleness and sensibility of a woman.
—JEFFERSONIAN POLITICAL OPERATIVE
AND NEWSPAPERMAN JAMES CALLENDER ON JOHN ADAMS

The moral character of Jefferson was repulsive. Continually puling
about liberty, equality and the degrading curse of slavery, he brought
his own children to the hammer, and money of his debaucheries.
—ALEXANDER HAMILTON

. . . Murder, robbery, rape, adultery and incest will be openly taught and
practiced, the air will be rent with the cries of distress, the soil soaked
with blood, and the nation black with crimes. Where is the heart that
can contemplate such a scene without shivering with horror?
—THE *NEW-ENGLAND COURANT*
ON THOMAS JEFFERSON'S CANDIDACY

Our churches will be prostrated, and some infamous prostitute, under the title of the Goddess of Reason, will preside in the Sanctuaries now devoted to the worship of the Most High.
—THE *NEW-ENGLAND PALLADIUM* FOLLOWING THOMAS JEFFERSON'S ELECTION

I never thought him an honest, frank-dealing man, but considered him as a crooked gun, . . . whose aim or shot you could never be sure of.
—THOMAS JEFFERSON ON AARON BURR

. . . a blooded, calculating unprincipled Usurper, without a virtue, no statesman, knowing nothing of commerce, political economy, or civil government, and supplying ignorance by bold presumption.
—THOMAS JEFFERSON ON NAPOLEON BONAPARTE

. . . as for Jemmy Madison—ah! Poor Jemmy!
He is but a withered little apple-John.
—WASHINGTON IRVING ON JAMES MADISON

. . . a commonplace man of no great brilliance.
—JOHN AND ALICE DURANT ON JAMES MONROE

●

His disposition is as perverse and mulish as that of his father.
—JAMES BUCHANAN ON JOHN QUINCY ADAMS

●

His face is livid, gaunt his whole body,

his breath is green with gall; his tongue drips poison.
—JOHN QUINCY ADAMS ON A POLITICAL OPPONENT

●

He is, like almost all the eminent men of this country, only half

educated. His morals, public and private, are loose.
—JOHN QUINCY ADAMS ON HENRY CLAY

●

. . . the panderer of an Autocrat.
—THE *NEW HAMPSHIRE PATRIOT*, ACCUSING
JOHN QUINCY ADAMS OF PROVIDING WOMEN FOR THE
CZAR WHEN ADAMS WAS AMBASSADOR TO RUSSIA

. . . a disgusting man to do business with. Coarse, dirty and clownish.
—WILLIAM HENRY HARRISON ON JOHN QUINCY ADAMS

. . . "a COMMON PROSTITUTE brought to this country
by British soldiers," and also that "she afterward married a
MULATTO MAN with whom she had several children,
of which General JACKSON IS ONE!"
—NEWSPAPER EDITOR, LAWYER, AND LEGISLATOR
CHARLES HAMMOND ON ANDREW JACKSON'S MOTHER

A barbarian who could not write a sentence of
grammar and hardly could spell his own name.
—JOHN QUINCY ADAMS ON ANDREW JACKSON

Ought a convicted adulteress and her paramour husband to be placed
in the highest offices of the free and Christian land?
—SUPPORTERS OF JOHN QUINCY ADAMS,
REFERRING TO ANDREW JACKSON'S MARRIAGE BEFORE
RACHEL JACKSON'S FORMER HUSBAND OBTAINED A DIVORCE

He is ignorant, passionate, hypocritical, corrupt and easily swayed by
the basest men who surround him.
—HENRY CLAY ON ANDREW JACKSON

•

He is certainly the basest, meanest scoundrel that ever disgraced the
image of God, nothing is too mean or low for him to condescend to.
—ANDREW JACKSON ON HENRY CLAY

•

I didn't shoot Henry Clay and I didn't hang John Calhoun.
—ANDREW JACKSON, COMMENTING ON THINGS HE HAD LEFT
UNDONE

•

Van Buren struts and swaggers like a crow in the gutter.
He is laced up in corsets. . . . It would be difficult to say,
from his personal appearance, whether he was a man or a woman.
—US REPRESENTATIVE DAVY CROCKETT ON MARTIN VAN BUREN

. . . the degenerate widower Van Buren had instructed groundskeepers to build for him, in back of the Executive Mansion, a large mound in the shape of a female breast, topped by a carefully landscaped nipple. Van Buren . . . was a depraved executive autocrat who oppressed the people by day and who, by night, violated the sanctity of the people's house with extravagant debaucheries—joined, some whispered, by the disgusting Vice President Johnson and his Negro harem.
—US CONGRESSMAN CHARLES OGLE ON MARTIN VAN BUREN

Our Present Imbecile Chief.
—ANDREW JACKSON ON WILLIAM HENRY HARRISON

Turnacoat Tyler.
—JOHN TYLER'S POLITICAL ENEMIES

He was the least conspicuous man
who had ever been nominated for president.
—CARL R. FISHER ON JAMES K. POLK

He is a bewildered, confounded, and miserably perplexed man.
—ABRAHAM LINCOLN ON JAMES K. POLK

Zachary Taylor's name seems more likely to appear as a Jeopardy!
question than on any list of presidential greats.
—CATHERINE CLINTON, HISTORIAN

. . . a funny-sounding, obscure, mid-nineteenth-century president.
—MARK KATZ ON MILLARD FILLMORE

Don't get me wrong. [Millard] Fillmore's been good for many a chuckle
over the years. It's just that most of the laughter has come at his
expense.
—BOB DOLE

He was another one that was a complete fizzle . . . Pierce
didn't know what was going on, and even if he had,
he wouldn't of known what to do about it.
—HARRY TRUMAN ON FRANKLIN PIERCE

. . . a bloated mass of political putridity.

—US CONGRESSMAN THADDEUS STEVENS ON JAMES BUCHANAN

He has been called a mediocre man; but this is unwarranted flattery.

He was a politician of monumental littleness.

—THEODORE ROOSEVELT ON JOHN TYLER

I have just read your dispatch about sore-tongued and fatigued horses.

Will you pardon me for asking what the horses of your army have done

since the battle of Antietam that fatigues anything?

—ABRAHAM LINCOLN IN A TELEGRAM
TO GENERAL GEORGE B. MCCLELLAN

The President is nothing more than a well-meaning baboon . . .

I went to the White House directly after tea where I found

the original Gorilla about as intelligent as ever.

What a specimen to be at the head of our affairs now!

—GENERAL GEORGE B. MCCLELLAN ON ABRAHAM LINCOLN

My dear McClellan: If you don't want to use the army I should like to borrow it for a while. Yours respectfully, A. Lincoln.
—ABRAHAM LINCOLN TO GENERAL GEORGE B. MCCLELLAN

•

Filthy Story-Teller, Despot, Liar, Thief, Braggart, Buffoon, Usurper, Monster, Ignoramus Abe, Old Scoundrel, Perjurer, Robber, Swindler, Tyrant, Field-Butcher, Land Pirate.
—A COLLECTION OF ANTI-LINCOLN EPITHETS THAT APPEARED IN *HARPER'S WEEKLY*

•

When he hits upon a policy, substantially good in itself, he contrives to belittle it, besmear it in some way to render it mean, contemptible and useless. Even wisdom from him seems but folly.
—THE *NEW YORK POST* ON ABRAHAM LINCOLN

. . . We did not conceive it possible that even Mr. Lincoln would produce a paper so slipshod, so loose-joined, so puerile, not alone in literary construction, but in its ideas, its sentiments, its grasp. He has outdone himself. He has literally come out of the little end of his own horn. By the side of it, mediocrity is superb.

—THE *CHICAGO TIMES*
COMMENTING ON THE GETTYSBURG ADDRESS

His argument is as thin as the . . . soup that was made by boiling the shadow of a pigeon that had been starved to death.

—ABRAHAM LINCOLN ON STEPHEN A. DOUGLAS

He can compress the most words
into the smallest idea of any man I know.

—ABRAHAM LINCOLN ON A POLITICAL OPPONENT

. . . [He could] drink more liquor than all the boys in town together.

—AMERICAN POLITICIAN STEPHEN A. DOUGLAS, WHO LOST
TO ABRAHAM LINCOLN IN 1860, ON ABRAHAM LINCOLN

God damn your god damned old hellfired god damned soul to hell god damn you and god damn your god damned family's god damned hellfired god damned soul to hell and good damnation god damn them and god damn your god damned friends to hell.

—PETER MUGGINS TO ABRAHAM LINCOLN

He is such an infernal liar.

—ULYSSES S. GRANT ON ANDREW JOHNSON

. . . a short, round-shouldered man, in a very tarnished uniform . . . no station, no manner . . . and a rather scrubby look withal.

—NEWSPAPER CORRESPONDENT CHARLES C. COFFIN
ON ULYSSES S. GRANT

His Fraudulency

—DEMOCRATIC PARTY NICKNAME FOR RUTHERFORD B. HAYES

Rutherfraud.

—ANOTHER DEMOCRATIC PARTY NICKNAME
FOR RUTHERFORD B. HAYES

Garfield has shown that he is not possessed
of the backbone of an angleworm.
—ULYSSES S. GRANT ON JAMES GARFIELD

· · ·

. . . a non-entity with side whiskers . . .
—WOODROW WILSON ON CHESTER A. ARTHUR

· · ·

Ma, Ma, where's my Pa? Going to the White House! Ha Ha Ha!
—REPUBLICAN PARTY ALLUSION TO THE CONTENTION THAT
GROVER CLEVELAND FATHERED AN ILLEGITIMATE
CHILD WHILE GOVERNOR OF NEW YORK

· · ·

He is a cold-blooded, narrow-minded, prejudiced, obstinate, timid old
psalm-singing Indianapolis politician.
—THEODORE ROOSEVELT ON BENJAMIN HARRISON

· · ·

Why, if a man were to call my dog McKinley, and the brute failed to
resent to the death the . . . insult, I'd drown it.
—JOURNALIST WILLIAM COWPER BRANN
ON WILLIAM MCKINLEY

He has no more backbone than a chocolate éclair.
—SPEAKER OF THE HOUSE THOMAS REED
ON WILLIAM MCKINLEY

I am told he no sooner thinks than he talks, which is a miracle not wholly in accord with an educational theory of forming an opinion.
—WOODROW WILSON ON THEODORE ROOSEVELT

An old maid with testosterone poisoning.
—HISTORIAN PATRICIA O'TOOLE ON THEODORE ROOSEVELT

He is the most dangerous man of the age.
—WOODROW WILSON ON THEODORE ROOSEVELT

[He is] a flub-dub with a streak of the second-rate and the common in him.
—THEODORE ROOSEVELT ON WILLIAM HOWARD TAFT

I regard him as a ruthless hypocrite and as an opportunist,
who has not convictions he would not barter at once for votes.
—WILLIAM HOWARD TAFT ON WOODROW WILSON

[He is a] Byzantine logothete.
—THEODORE ROOSEVELT ON WOODROW WILSON
(THE PHRASE MEANS "GLORIFIED ACCOUNTANT.")

. . . [an] infernal skunk in the White House.
—THEODORE ROOSEVELT ON WOODROW WILSON

A little emasculated mass of inanity.
—THEODORE ROOSEVELT ON AUTHOR HENRY JAMES

When he tackled the trusts the thing that he had in his mind's eye was
not the restoration of competition but the subordination of all private
trusts to one great national trust, with himself at its head. And when he
attacked the courts it was not because they put their own prejudice before
the law but because they refused to put his prejudices before the law.
—H. L. MENCKEN ON THEODORE ROOSEVELT

Mr. Wilson bores me with his Fourteen Points; why,
God Almighty has only ten.
—GEORGES CLEMENCEAU ON WOODROW WILSON

•

He has a bungalow mind.
—WOODROW WILSON ON WARREN G. HARDING

•

It reminds me of a string of wet sponges; it reminds me of tattered washing on the line; it reminds me of stale bean soup, of college yells, of dogs barking idiotically through endless nights. It is so bad that a sort of grandeur creeps into it. It drags itself out of the dark abysm of pish, and crawls insanely up the topmost pinnacle of posh. It is rumble and bumble. It is flap and doodle. It is balder and dash.
—H. L. MENCKEN ON WARREN G. HARDING'S WRITING STYLE

•

His speeches leave the impression of an army of pompous phrases moving over the landscape in search of an idea.
—SENATOR WILLIAM MCADOO ON WARREN G. HARDING

. . . the only man, woman, or child who wrote a simple declarative
sentence with seven grammatical errors is dead.
—E. E. CUMMINGS ON WARREN G. HARDING

He looks as though he's been weaned on a pickle.
—POLITICAL HOSTESS AND PRESIDENTIAL DAUGHTER ALICE
ROOSEVELT LONGWORTH ON CALVIN COOLIDGE

He slept more than any other president, whether by day or night.
Nero fiddled, but Coolidge only snored.
—H. L. MENCKEN ON CALVIN COOLIDGE

How can they tell?
—DOROTHY PARKER, LEARNING OF CALVIN COOLIDGE'S DEATH

That man has offered me unsolicited advice for six years, all of it bad.
—CALVIN COOLIDGE ON HERBERT HOOVER

He wouldn't commit himself to the time
of day from a hatful of watches.
—JOURNALIST WESTBROOK PEGLER ON HERBERT HOOVER

●

Such a little man could not have made so big a depression.
—SIX-TIME SOCIALIST PARTY PRESIDENTIAL CANDIDATE
NORMAN THOMAS ON HERBERT HOOVER

●

. . . [a] chameleon on plaid.
—HERBERT HOOVER ON FRANKLIN D. ROOSEVELT

●

If he became convinced tomorrow that coming out for cannibalism
would get him the votes he sorely needs, he would begin fattening a
missionary in the White House backyard come Wednesday.
—H. L. MENCKEN ON FRANKLIN D. ROOSEVELT

●

Franklin Roosevelt had refused to lift a finger to help the outgoing
administration relieve the suffering of the Depression, so he could draw
a starker contrast with President Hoover after his own inauguration.
—FORMER SECRETARY OF THE TREASURY TIMOTHY GEITHNER

To err is Truman.
—A POPULAR JOKE IN 1948,
THE YEAR OF HARRY S. TRUMAN'S ELECTION

●

Ike didn't know anything, and all the time he was in office, he didn't learn a thing. . . . The general doesn't know any more about politics than a pig knows about Sunday.
—HARRY S. TRUMAN ON DWIGHT D. EISENHOWER

●

I didn't fire him because he was a dumb son of a bitch, although he was, but that's not against the law for generals.
—HARRY S. TRUMAN ON GENERAL DOUGLAS MACARTHUR

●

I've read your review of my daughter Margaret's concert last night and I've come to the conclusion that you're an eight-ulcer man on a four ulcer pay. And after reading such poppycock, it's obvious that you're off the beam and that at least four of your ulcers are working overtime. I hope to meet you and when I do, you're going to need a new nose, plenty of beefsteak for black eyes, and perhaps a supporter below.
—HARRY S. TRUMAN, TO A NEWSPAPER MUSIC CRITIC

If there had been any formidable body of cannibals in the country, he
would have promised to provide them with free missionaries fattened
at the taxpayers' expense.
—H. L. MENCKEN ON HARRY S. TRUMAN

As an intellectual he bestowed upon the games of golf
and bridge all the enthusiasm and perseverance that
he withheld from books and ideas.
—PRESIDENTIAL AIDE AND SPEECHWRITER EMMET HUGHES
ON DWIGHT D. EISENHOWER

You can always tell a Harvard man but you can't tell him much.
—DWIGHT D. EISENHOWER ON JOHN F. KENNEDY
(THE LINE DID NOT ORIGINATE WITH EISENHOWER.)

How can a guy this politically immature
seriously expect to be President?
—FRANKLIN D. ROOSEVELT JR. ON JOHN F. KENNEDY

The Wizard of Ooze
—JOHN F. KENNEDY ON SPEAKER
OF THE HOUSE EVERETT DIRKSEN

•

[He was the] enviably attractive nephew who sings an Irish
ballad for the company and then winsomely disappears
before the table clearing and dishwashing begin.
—LYNDON B. JOHNSON ON JOHN F. KENNEDY

•

The CIA is made up of boys whose families sent them to Princeton but
wouldn't let them into the family brokerage business.
—LYNDON B. JOHNSON ON THE CENTRAL
INTELLIGENCE AGENCY

•

All that Hubert needs over there is a gal to answer the phone and a
pencil with an eraser on it.
—LYNDON B. JOHNSON ON HUBERT HUMPHREY

Jerry Ford is so dumb he can't fart and chew gum at the same time.
—LYNDON B. JOHNSON ON GERALD R. FORD

Ford's economics are the worst thing that's happened to this country since panty hose ruined finger-f**king.
—LYNDON B. JOHNSON ON GERALD R. FORD

Jack the Zipper
—POPULAR REFERENCE TO JOHN F. KENNEDY'S EXTRAMARITAL AFFAIRS

He turned out to be so many different characters he could have populated all of *War and Peace* and still had a few people left over.
—AUTHOR AND JOURNALIST HERBERT MITGANG ABOUT LYNDON B. JOHNSON

If you give me a week, I might think of one.
—DWIGHT D. EISENHOWER, AFTER BEING ASKED WHETHER
VICE PRESIDENT RICHARD NIXON HAD CONTRIBUTED ANY
MAJOR IDEAS TO EISENHOWER'S PRESIDENCY

Nixon is a purposeless man, but I have great faith in his cowardice.
—JOURNALIST JIMMY BRESLIN

He inherited some good instincts from his Quaker forebears,
but by diligent hard work, he overcame them.
—JOURNALIST JAMES RESTON ON RICHARD NIXON

A hypocrite is the kind of politician who would cut down a redwood
tree and then mount the stump to make a speech for conservation.
—POLITICIAN ADLAI STEVENSON ON RICHARD NIXON

Would you buy a second-hand car from this man?
—SAID OF RICHARD NIXON;
ATTRIBUTED TO HUMORIST MORT SAHL

He can lie out of both sides of his mouth at the same time, and if he ever caught himself telling the truth, he'd lie just to keep his hand in.
—HARRY S. TRUMAN ON RICHARD NIXON

Avoid all needle drugs. The only dope worth shooting is Richard Nixon.
—ABBIE HOFFMAN

He's a nice guy, but he played too much football with his helmet off.
—LYNDON B. JOHNSON ON GERALD R. FORD

In the Bob Hope Classic, the participation of President Gerald Ford was more than enough to remind you that the nuclear button was at one stage at the disposal of a man who might have either pressed it by mistake or else pressed it deliberately in order to obtain room service.
—CLIVE JAMES

History buffs probably noted the reunion at a Washington party a few weeks ago of three ex-presidents: Carter, Ford, and Nixon—See No Evil, Hear No Evil, and Evil.

—BOB DOLE

He is your typical, smiling, brilliant, back-stabbing, bullshitting Southern nut-cutter.

—LABOR LEADER LANE KIRKWOOD ON JIMMY CARTER

What makes him think a middle-aged actor, who's played with a chimp, could have a future in politics?

—RONALD REAGAN ON CLINT EASTWOOD'S CARMEL, CALIFORNIA, MAYORAL BID

[He is] A triumph of the embalmer's art.

—GORE VIDAL ON RONALD REAGAN

He's proof that there's life after death.
—MORT SAHL ON RONALD REAGAN

The battle for the mind of Ronald Reagan was like the
trench warfare of World War I: never have so many
fought so hard for such barren terrain.
—PEGGY NOONAN, PRESIDENTIAL SPEECHWRITER
AND JOURNALIST, ON RONALD REAGAN

I believe that Ronald Reagan can make this country what it once
was—an Arctic region covered with ice.
—COMEDIAN STEVE MARTIN

Ronald Reagan doesn't dye his hair, he's just prematurely orange.
—GERALD R. FORD ON RONALD REAGAN

•

I think Nancy does most of his talking; you'll notice that she never drinks water when Ronnie speaks.
—ROBIN WILLIAMS ON RONALD REAGAN

•

Washington could not tell a lie; Nixon could not tell the truth; Reagan cannot tell the difference.
—MORT SAHL

•

I have been disappointed in almost everything he has done.
—JIMMY CARTER ON GEORGE H. W. BUSH

•

[A] hustler from Chicago.
—GEORGE H. W. BUSH ON THE REVEREND JESSE JACKSON

When I was president, I said I was a Ford, not a Lincoln. Well, what we have now is a convertible Dodge.

—GERALD R. FORD ON BILL CLINTON

I have never seen . . . so slippery, so disgusting a candidate.

—JOURNALIST NAT HENTOFF ON BILL CLINTON

Sadly, I don't think the Clintons are progressives, or liberals. I think it's far more dangerous than this. I think these people are amoral thieves. I mean, they would steal a hot stove. They really will do anything for money, and I think that will, in many key ways, be their downfall.

—POLITICAL CONSULTANT ROGER STONE
ON BILL AND HILLARY CLINTON

I wouldn't want any unneutered Clintons in my house.

—AUTHOR AND RADIO TALK SHOW HOST LINDA CHAVEZ,
SPECULATING ON THE REPRODUCTIVE STATUS
OF THE CLINTONS' CAT, SOCKS

Hell, if you work for Bill Clinton, you go up and down more times than a whore's nightgown.
—JAMES CARVILLE, POLITICAL COMMENTATOR

Bill Clinton's foreign policy experience is pretty much confined to having had breakfast once at the International House of Pancakes.
—PAT BUCHANAN, POLITICAL COLUMNIST
AND COMMENTATOR, ON BILL CLINTON

What is his accomplishment? That he's no longer an obnoxious drunk?
—RON REAGAN JR. ON GEORGE W. BUSH

People might cite George Bush as proof that you can be totally impervious to the effects of Harvard and Yale education.
—FORMER CONGRESSMAN BARNEY FRANK ON GEORGE W. BUSH

He can't help it—he was born with a silver foot in his mouth.
—ANN RICHARDS ON GEORGE W. BUSH

[He is] logically unsound, confused and unprincipled,
unwise to the extreme.
—FORMER CHINESE COMMUNIST PARTY OFFICIAL
JIANG ZEMIN ON GEORGE W. BUSH

If ignorance ever goes to $40 a barrel, I want
drilling rights on George Bush's head.
—POLITICAL ACTIVIST AND COLUMNIST JIM HIGHTOWER
ON GEORGE W. BUSH

Calling George Bush shallow is like calling a dwarf short.
—MOLLY IVINS ON GEORGE W. BUSH

Hopefully, he is not as stupid as he seems, nor as Mafia-like as his
predecessors were.
—FIDEL CASTRO ON GEORGE W. BUSH

Bush is smart. I don't think that Bush will ever be impeached, 'cause unlike Clinton, Reagan, or even his father, George W. is immune from scandal. Because, if George W. testifies that he had no idea what was going on, wouldn't you believe him?

—JAY LENO

Bush/Cheney '04: Putting the "Con" in Conservative.

—CAMPAIGN BUMPER STICKER

Bush the younger has two things going for him that his father never had. One: an easy charm with regular people and two: the power to make them disappear without a trial.

—BILL MAHER

You lie!

—REPRESENTATIVE JOE WILSON SHOUTING AT BARACK OBAMA DURING A JOINT SESSION OF CONGRESS

I don't care where he's from. We are looking at a forged document.
—SHERIFF JOE ARPAIO ON BARACK OBAMA'S BIRTH
CERTIFICATE SHOWING THAT HE WAS BORN IN HAWAII
(THE SO-CALLED "BIRTHER" ISSUE ALLEGING THAT
OBAMA WAS BORN IN KENYA)

Obamacare is Obama fraud. "You can keep your doctor. You can keep your insurance." Lie. Lie. . . . "It's gonna save you money." Big lie.
—RUDOLPH GIULIANI ON BARACK OBAMA'S
AFFORDABLE CARE ACT

Gov. Romney doesn't have a five-point plan; he has a one-point plan. And that plan is to make sure that folks at the top play by a different set of rules.
—BARACK OBAMA ON MITT ROMNEY
DURING A PRESIDENTIAL DEBATE

When Mexico sends its people, they're not sending their best. They're not sending you. They're not sending you. They're sending people that have lots of problems, and they're bringing those problems with us. They're bringing drugs. They're bringing crime. They're rapists. And some, I assume, are good people.

—DONALD J. TRUMP ANNOUNCING HIS CANDIDACY

Crooked Hillary. Lying crooked Hillary.

—DONALD J. TRUMP'S EPITHETS FOR HILLARY R. CLINTON DURING THEIR PRESIDENTIAL CAMPAIGNS

Donald was one of the people who rooted for the housing crisis, that's called business, by the way.

—HILLARY CLINTON REFERRING TO DONALD J. TRUMP

Our weak president, that kisses everybody's ass, is in more wars than I have ever seen. Now he's in Libya, he's in Afghanistan, he's in Iraq. Nobody respects us.

—DONALD J. TRUMP ON BARACK OBAMA

[He is] unfit to serve . . . and woefully unprepared to do this job.
—BARACK OBAMA ON DONALD J. TRUMP

•

[He is] the worst president, maybe in the history of our country.
—DONALD J. TRUMP ON BARACK OBAMA

Chapter

· · · · · · · · · · · ·

II

Political Mudslinging . . . and Worse

You have all the characteristics of a popular politician: a horrible
voice, bad breeding, and a vulgar manner.
—ARISTOPHANES

●

Reader, suppose you were an idiot; and suppose you were
a member of Congress; but I repeat myself.
—MARK TWAIN

●

He was no better than the common cold.
—HARRY TRUMAN ON HAROLD ICKES

●

He's as ambitious as Lucifer, cold as a snake and
what he touches will not prosper.
—SAM HOUSTON ON JEFFERSON DAVIS

●

They never open their mouths without subtracting
from the sum of human knowledge.
—THOMAS REED OF TWO FELLOW CONGRESSMEN

He puts the "goober" in "gubernatorial."
—POLITICAL ACTIVIST AND COLUMNIST
JIM HIGHTOWER ON TEXAS GOVERNOR RICK PERRY

[He is] a rigid, fanatic, ambitious, selfish partisan, and sectional
turncoat with too much genius and too little common sense,
who will either die a traitor or a madman.
—HENRY CLAY ON JOHN C. CALHOUN

He appears to have been called "The Little Giant" more because he
was little than because he was a giant.
—IRVING STONE ON STEVEN A. DOUGLAS

He is racist, he's homophobic, he's xenophobic and he's a sexist. He's
the perfect Republican candidate.
—RADIO TALK SHOW HOST BILL PRESS ON PAT BUCHANAN

I could carve out of a banana a judge with more backbone than that.
—THEODORE ROOSEVELT ON SUPREME COURT JUSTICE
OLIVER WENDELL HOLMES

She's got dyed blonde hair and pouty lips, and a steely blue stare, like a
sadistic nurse in a mental hospital.
—BORIS JOHNSON ON HILLARY CLINTON

•

To just be grossly generalistic, you can put half of Trump supporters
into what I call the basket of deplorables. Right? Racist, sexist,
homophobic, xenophobic, Islamaphobic, you name it.
—HILLARY CLINTON

•

Senator, I served with Jack Kennedy. I knew Jack Kennedy. Jack
Kennedy was a friend of mine. Senator, you're no Jack Kennedy.
**—1988 VICE-PRESIDENTIAL CANDIDATE
LLOYD BENTSEN TO DAN QUAYLE**

As to Burr there is nothing in his favour. His private character is not defended by his most partial friends. He is bankrupt beyond redemption except by the plunder of his country. His public principles have no other spring or aim than his own aggrandisement per fas et nefas. If he can, he will certainly disturb our institutions to secure to himself permanent power and with it wealth. He is truly the Cataline of America—& if I may credit Major Wilcocks, he has held very vindictive language respecting his opponents.

—ALEXANDER HAMILTON ON AARON BURR

Any political party that can't cough up anything better than a treacherous brain-damaged old vulture like Hubert Humphrey deserves every beating it gets. They don't hardly make 'em like Hubert any more—but just to be on the safe side, he should be castrated anyway.

—HUNTER S. THOMPSON ON HUBERT H. HUMPHREY

[He is] an empty suit that goes to funerals and plays golf.

—BUSINESSMAN AND PRESIDENTIAL CANDIDATE
ROSS PEROT ON DAN QUAYLE

Hubert Humphrey talks so fast that listening to him is like trying to
read *Playboy* magazine with your wife turning the pages.
—BARRY GOLDWATER ON HUBERT H. HUMPHREY

•

. . . the most meanly and foolishly treacherous man I ever heard of.
—JAMES RUSSELL LOWELL ON DANIEL WEBSTER

•

The word liberty in the mouth of Mr. Webster sounds like
the word love in the mouth of a courtesan.
—RALPH WALDO EMERSON ON DANIEL WEBSTER

•

He has all the characteristics of a dog except loyalty.
—SAM HOUSTON ON LEGISLATOR THOMAS JEFFERSON GREEN

When he does smile, he looks as if he's just evicted a widow.
—JOURNALIST MIKE ROYKO ON BOB DOLE

We need segregated buses . . . This is Obama's America.
—RUSH LIMBAUGH

. . . a left-leaning marshmallow . . .
—BOB DOLE ON RAMSEY CLARK

He's the only man able to walk under a bed without hitting his head.
—RADIO AND NEWSPAPER JOURNALIST WALTER WINCHELL
ON THOMAS E. DEWEY

You really have to get to know him to dislike him.
—HISTORIAN JAMES T. PATTERSON ON THOMAS E. DEWEY

He is just about the nastiest little man I've ever known.
He struts sitting down.
—LILLIAN DYKSTRA ON THOMAS E. DEWEY

His mind was like a soup dish, wide and shallow; it could hold a small
amount of nearly anything, but the slightest jarring spilled the soup
into somebody's lap.
—IRVING STONE ON WILLIAM JENNINGS BRYAN

He's thin, boys. He's thin as piss on a hot rock.
—SENATOR WILLIAM F. JENNER ON W. AVERELL HARRIMAN

Marion Barry at the Million Man March—you know what that means?

That means even at our finest hour, we had a crackhead on stage.

—CHRIS ROCK ON MARION BARRY, THE WASHINGTON, DC,
MAYOR JAILED FOR USING CRACK COCAINE

He is suffering from halitosis of the intellect.

That's presuming he has intellect.

—HAROLD ICKES ON LOUISIANA GOVERNOR HUEY LONG

It was hard to listen to Goldwater and realize that a man could be half
Jewish and yet sometimes appear twice as dense as the normal Gentile.

—I. F. STONE ON SENATOR BARRY GOLDWATER

In a recent fire Bob Dole's library burned down. Both books were lost.

And he hadn't even finished coloring one of them.

—JACK KEMP, CONGRESSMAN AND DOLE'S POLITICAL RIVAL

Patton's mouth does not always carry out the functions of his brain.
—GENERAL WALTER BEDELL SMITH ON
GENERAL GEORGE PATTON

Never trust a man who combs his hair straight from his left armpit.
—ALICE ROOSEVELT LONGWORTH ON
GENERAL DOUGLAS MACARTHUR

MacArthur is the type of man who thinks that when he gets to heaven,
God will step down from the great white throne and bow him into his
vacated seat.
—HAROLD ICKES ON GENERAL DOUGLAS MACARTHUR

The General is suffering from mental saddle sores.
—HAROLD ICKES ON HUGH S. JOHNSON

British Prime Ministers, Politicians, and Their Critics:

He is one of those orators of whom it was well said. Before they get up,
they do not know what they are going to say; when they are speaking,
they do not know what they are saying; and when they have sat down,
they do not know what they have said.

—SIR WINSTON CHURCHILL ON LORD CHARLES BERESFORD

I remember when I was a child, being taken to the celebrated Barnum's
Circus, which contained an exhibition of freaks and monstrosities,
but the exhibit on the programme which I most desired to see was the
one described as "The Boneless Wonder." My parents judged that the
spectacle would be too demoralising and revolting for my youthful eye
and I have waited fifty years, to see the Boneless Wonder sitting on the
Treasury Bench.

**—SIR WINSTON CHURCHILL ON FORMER
PRIME MINISTER RAMSAY MACDONALD**

We know that he has, more than any other man,

the gift of compressing the largest amount of words

into the smallest amount of thought.

—SIR WINSTON CHURCHILL ON RAMSAY MACDONALD

•

Unless the right honourable gentleman changes his policy and

methods and moves without the slightest delay, he will be as great a

curse to this country in peace as he was a squalid nuisance in time of

war.

—SIR WINSTON CHURCHILL ON ANEURIN BEVAN

•

. . . a sheep in sheep's clothing . . .

—SIR WINSTON CHURCHILL ON FORMER PRIME MINISTER

CLEMENT ATTLEE

There but for the grace of God, goes God.

—SIR WINSTON CHURCHILL ON SIR STAFFORD CRIPPS

•

I wish Stanley Baldwin no ill, but it would have been much better if he had never lived.

—SIR WINSTON CHURCHILL ON FORMER PRIME MINISTER STANLEY BALDWIN

•

He looked at foreign affairs through the wrong end of a municipal drainpipe.

—SIR WINSTON CHURCHILL ON FORMER PRIME MINISTER NEVILLE CHAMBERLAIN

In defeat unbeatable, in victory unbearable.
—SIR WINSTON CHURCHILL ON GENERAL BERNARD
MONTGOMERY

•

A bloodthirsty guttersnipe, a monster of wickedness,
insatiable in his lust for blood and plunder.
—SIR WINSTON CHURCHILL ON ADOLPH HITLER

•

Tell His Lordship I'm sealed on the privy and
can only deal with one shit at a time.
—SIR WINSTON CHURCHILL, FROM THE
LAVATORY AFTER BEING TOLD THAT THE
LORD PRIVY SEAL WISHED TO SPEAK TO HIM

If [Prime Minister William] Gladstone fell into the Thames,
that would be a misfortune; and if anybody pulled
him out, that would be a calamity.
—BENJAMIN DISRAELI, ON THE DIFFERENCE
BETWEEN A MISFORTUNE AND A CALAMITY

•

He has not one single redeeming defect.
—BENJAMIN DISRAELI ON PRIME MINISTER WILLIAM
GLADSTONE

•

It was said Mr. Gladstone could convince most people
of most things, and himself of anything.
—DEAN WILLIAM INGE ON WILLIAM GLADSTONE

[He is] inebriated with the exuberance of his own verbosity,
and gifted with an egotistical imagination.
—BENJAMIN DISRAELI ON WILLIAM GLADSTONE

The right honourable gentleman is reminiscent of a poker. The only
difference is that a poker gives off the occasional signs of warmth.
—BENJAMIN DISRAELI ON SIR ROBERT PEEL

He is a great master of gibes and flouts and jeers.
—BENJAMIN DISRAELI ON LORD SALISBURY

A conservative government is an organised hypocrisy.
— **BENJAMIN DISRAELI ON SIR ROBERT PEEL'S GOVERNMENT**

The Tories always hold the view that the state is an apparatus
for the protection of the swag of the property owners . . . Christ
drove the money changers out of the temple, but you inscribe
their title deed on the altar cloth.
— **ANEURIN BEVAN TO SIR WINSTON CHURCHILL**

He is a man suffering from petrified adolescence.
— **ANEURIN BEVAN ON SIR WINSTON CHURCHILL**

Listening to a speech by Chamberlain is like paying a visit to
Woolworth's: everything in its place and nothing above sixpence.
— **ANEURIN BEVAN ON NEVILLE CHAMBERLAIN**

He seems determined to make a trumpet sound like a tin whistle. He brings to the fierce struggle of politics the tepid enthusiasm of a lazy summer afternoon at a cricket match.
—ANEURIN BEVAN ON CLEMENT ATTLEE

No amount of cajolery, and no attempts at ethical or social seduction, can eradicate from my heart a deep burning hatred of the Tory party. So far as I am concerned, they are lower than vermin.
—ANEURIN BEVAN ON THE CONSERVATIVE PARTY

Tory shame was only slightly alleviated by Walter Monckton, and then they didn't know whether to wear him as a gas mask or a jock strap.
—ANEURIN BEVAN ON CABINET MINISTER WALTER MONCKTON

He has the lucidity which is the byproduct of a fundamentally sterile mind.
—ANEURIN BEVAN ON NEVILLE CHAMBERLAIN

I am not going to spend any time whatsoever in attacking the Foreign Secretary. If we complain about the tune, there is no need to attack the monkey when the organ grinder is present.

—ANEURIN BEVAN ON PRIME MINISTER ANTHONY
EDEN AND FOREIGN SECRETARY SELWYN LLOYD

He is a mere cork, dancing in a current which he cannot control.

—PRIME MINISTER ARTHUR BALFOUR
ON PRIME MINISTER HENRY CAMPBELL-BANNERMAN

. . . a body of five men chosen at random
from amongst the unemployed.

—DAVID LLOYD GEORGE ON THE HOUSE OF LORDS

. . . wild men, screaming through the keyholes.

—DAVID LLOYD GEORGE ON THE VERSAILLES
PEACE CONFERENCE DELEGATES

His impact on history will be no more than the
whiff of scent on a lady's handkerchief.
—DAVID LLOYD GEORGE ON FORMER
PRIME MINISTER ARTHUR BALFOUR

Neville has a retail mind in a wholesale business.
—DAVID LLOYD GEORGE ON NEVILLE CHAMBERLAIN

The Prime Minister should give an example of sacrifice,
because there is nothing that can contribute more to
victory than he should sacrifice the seals of office.
—DAVID LLOYD GEORGE ON NEVILLE CHAMBERLAIN

You don't reach Downing Street by pretending you've travelled the
road to Damascus when you haven't even left home.
—MARGARET THATCHER ON LABOUR
PARTY LEADER NEIL KINNOCK

As usual the Liberals offer a mixture of sound and
original ideas. Unfortunately none of the sound ideas
is original and none of the original ideas is sound.
—FORMER PRIME MINISTER HAROLD MACMILLAN
ON THE LIBERAL PARTY

He was the future once.
—BRITISH PRIME MINISTER DAVID CAMERON
ON FORMER PRIME MINISTER TONY BLAIR

My one ardent desire is that after the war he should be publicly
castrated in front of Nurse Cavell's statue.
—AUTHOR AND CRITIC LYTTON STRACHEY
ON DAVID LLOYD GEORGE

Gladstone appears to me one of the contemptibilist men I ever looked
on. A poor Ritualist; almost spectral kind of phantasm of a man.
—THOMAS CARLYLE ON WILLIAM GLADSTONE

His smile was like the silver plate on a coffin.
—IRISH POLITICIAN JOHN PHILPOTT CURRAN
ON SIR ROBERT PEEL

He can't see a belt without hitting below it.
—MARGOT ASQUITH ON DAVID LLOYD GEORGE

. . . [He has] The manners of a cad and the tongue of a bargee.
—PRIME MINISTER HERBERT ASQUITH
ON STATESMAN JOSEPH CHAMBERLAIN

Attila the Hen
—BROADCASTER AND WRITER CLEMENT FREUD
ON MARGARET THATCHER

The Immaculate Misconception
—POLITICAN AND AUTHOR NORMAN ST JOHN-STEVAS
ON MARGARET THATCHER

She is a half-mad old bag lady.
—LABOUR MEMBER OF PARLIAMENT MUSICIAN TONY BANKS
ON MARGARET THATCHER

She sounded like the Book of Revelations read out
over a railway station public address system by a
headmistress of a certain age wearing calico knickers.
—CLIVE JAMES ON MARGARET THATCHER

The Prime Minister tells us she has given the French president a piece
of her mind, not a gift I would receive with alacrity.
—CABINET MEMBER DENIS HEALEY ON MARGARET THATCHER

She probably thinks Sinai is the plural of sinus.
—CABINET MINISTER JONATHAN AITKEN
ON MARGARET THATCHER

Tony Blair is the ultimate air guitarist of modern political rhetoric.
—POLITICAL COMMENTATOR AND WRITER WILL SELF

It is appalling that these ignorant and irresponsible men should be
cutting Asia Minor to bits as if they were dividing a cake . . .
—HAROLD NICOLSON ON GEORGES CLEMENCEAU,
DAVID LLOYD GEORGE, AND WOODROW WILSON

●

The Right Honourable Gentleman is indebted to his memory for his
jests and to his imagination for his facts.
—RICHARD BRINSLEY SHERIDAN ON THE EARL OF DUNDAS

●

He was oppressed by metaphor, dislocated by parentheses,
and debilitated by amplification.
—POLITICAL WRITER SAMUEL PARR ON WRITER
AND STATESMAN EDMUND BURKE

●

. . . [He is] Dangerous as an enemy, untrustworthy as a friend,
but fatal as a colleague.
—SIR HERCULES ROBINSON ON STATESMAN
JOSEPH CHAMBERLAIN

Oh, if I could piss the way he speaks!
—GEORGES CLEMENCEAU ON DAVID LLOYD GEORGE

One could not even dignify him with the name of stuffed shirt.
He was simply a hole on the air.
—GEORGE ORWELL ON BRITISH STATESMAN STANLEY BALDWIN

He has devoted the best years of his life to preparing
his impromptu speeches.
—EARL OF BIRKENHEAD ON SIR WINSTON CHURCHILL

He would kill his own mother just so that he could use her skin to
make a drum to beat his own praises.
—MARGOT ASQUITH ON SIR WINSTON CHURCHILL

He is a self-made man and worships his creator.
—STATESMAN JOHN BRIGHT ON BENJAMIN DISRAELI

I wouldn't spit in their mouths if their teeth were on fire.

**—TRADE UNION LEADER RODNEY BICKERSTAFFE
ON PRIME MINISTER JOHN MAJOR AND
CONSERVATIVE PARTY LEADER NORMAN LAMONT**

It might be nice to think that if Gordon Brown had read fewer books on political economy and American history, and more poetry, he would have been a less disastrous prime minister. But the heartiest diet of Emily Dickinson and William Allingham could not have loosened the knot of aggressive melancholy that made his character so unequal to his chosen vocation.

—JOURNALIST CHRISTOPHER HOWSE

And Other Political Figures:

The honorable member is living proof that a pig's bladder on a stick can be elected to Parliament.

**—LABOUR MEMBER OF PARLIAMENT TONY BANKS
ON CONSERVATIVE MP TERRY DICKS**

To make things worse, the Tories have elected a foetus as leader. I bet a
lot of them wish they had not voted against abortion now.
—LABOUR MEMBER OF PARLIAMENT TONY BANKS ON
CONSERVATIVE MP WILLIAM HAGUE

•

He lived a hypocrite and died a traitor.
—MEMBER OF PARLIAMENT JOHN FOSTER
ON OLIVER CROMWELL

Canadian Political Figures:

Canada has at last produced a political leader worthy of assassination.
—POET IRVING LAYTON ON CANADIAN
PRIME MINISTER PIERRE TRUDEAU

•

It is better to be sincere in one language than to be a twit in two.
—CANADIAN TRANSPORT MINISTER
JOHN CROSBIE ABOUT PIERRE TRUDEAU

•

The Honourable Member disagrees. I can hear him shaking his head.
—PIERRE TRUDEAU, REPLYING TO A QUESTION IN PARLIAMENT

Little chubby little sucker.
—CANADIAN REFORM MEMBER OF PARLIAMENT
DARREL STINSON ABOUT PROGRESSIVE CONSERVATIVE
LEADER JEAN CHAREST

Frankly, if I was going to recruit somebody,
I'd go further up the gene pool.
—CANADIAN LIBERAL CABINET MINISTER REG ALCOCK WHEN
ASKED WHETHER HE OFFERED AN AMBASSADORSHIP TO
CONSERVATIVE MEMBER OF PARLIAMENT INKY MARK

I've been called worse things by better men.
—FORMER CANADIAN PRIME MINISTER PIERRE TRUDEAU,
HEARING THAT RICHARD NIXON CALLED HIM "AN ASSHOLE."

British Royalty:

Strip your Louis Quatorze of his king gear, and there is left
nothing but a poor forked radish with a head fantastically carved.
—THOMAS CARLYLE ON KING LOUIS XIV OF FRANCE

. . . A pig, an ass, a dunghill, the spawn of an adder, a basilisk, a lying
buffoon, a mad fool with a frothy mouth.
—**MARTIN LUTHER ON KING HENRY VIII**

Henry VIII perhaps approached as nearly to the ideal standard of
perfect wickedness as the infirmities of human nature will allow.
—**POLITICIAN AND HISTORIAN SIR JAMES MACINTOSH**

. . . The plain truth is, that he was a most intolerable ruffian, a disgrace
to human nature, and a blot of blood and grease upon the history
of England.
—**CHARLES DICKENS ON KING HENRY VIII**

You have sent me a Flanders mare.
—**KING HENRY VIII ON SEEING HIS FOURTH WIFE,
ANNE OF CLEVES, FOR THE FIRST TIME**

. . . As just and merciful as Nero and as good
a Christian as Mohammed.
—JOHN WESLEY ON QUEEN ELIZABETH I

•

I cannot find it in me to fear a man who took ten
years a-learning of his alphabet.
—QUEEN ELIZABETH I ON KING PHILIP II OF SPAIN

•

. . . The most notorious whore in all the world.
—PURITAN LEADER SIR PETER WENTWORTH
ON MARY QUEEN OF SCOTS

•

. . . The wisest fool in Christendom.
—KING HENRI IV OF FRANCE ON KING JAMES I

No danger. For no man in England would take away
my life to make you king.
—KING CHARLES II TO HIS BROTHER THE
DUKE OF YORK AFTER THE DUKE WARNED HIM
OF THE DANGER OF TRAVELING UNPROTECTED

That is very true, for my words are my own,
but my actions are my ministers.
—KING CHARLES II TO THE EARL OF ROCHESTER,
WHO SUGGESTED THAT THE KING'S EPITAPH MIGHT
BE, "HERE LIES OUR SOVEREIGN LORD, THE KING,
WHOSE WORD NO MAN RELIES ON, WHO NEVER
SAID A FOOLISH THING, AND NEVER DID A WISE ONE."

She was happy as the dey was long.
—LORD NORBURY ON QUEEN CAROLINE'S
AFFAIR WITH THE DEY OF ALGIERS

My dear firstborn is the greatest ass, and the greatest liar and the greatest canaille and the greatest beast in the whole world and I most heartily wish he were out of it.
—QUEEN CAROLINE ON HER SON FREDERICK, PRINCE OF WALES

Here lies Fred, Who was alive and now is dead: Had it been his father, I had much rather; Had it been his brother, Better than another; Had it been his sister, No one would have missed her; Had it been the whole generation, Better for the nation: But since 'tis only Fred, Who was alive and is dead—There's no more to be said.
—HORACE WALPOLE ON FREDERICK, PRINCE OF WALES

. . . An Adonis of fifty . . . a violator of his word, a libertine over head and ears in debt and disgrace, a despiser of domestic ties, the companion of gamblers and demi-reps, a man without a single claim to the gratitude of his country or the respect of posterity . . .
—LEIGH HUNT ON THE PRINCE OF WALES, LATER GEORGE IV

A more contemptible, cowardly, selfish unfeeling dog does
not exist than this king . . . with vices and weaknesses of
the lowest and most contemptible order.

—DIARIST CHARLES GREVILLE ON KING GEORGE IV

•

Who's your fat friend?

—GEORGE BEAU BRUMMELL [TO A COMPANION],
REFERRING TO GEORGE IV

•

George the First was always reckoned Vile, but viler George the
Second; And what mortal ever heard any good from George the Third?
When from Earth the Fourth descended (God be praised!) the
Georges ended.

—WALTER SAVAGE LANDOR ON THE FIRST
FOUR ENGLISH KING GEORGES

Nowadays a parlor maid as ignorant as Queen Victoria was when she
came to the throne would be classed as mentally defective.
— GEORGE BERNARD SHAW

•

Born into the ranks of the working class, the new King's most likely
fate would have been that of a street-corner loafer.
— JAMES KEIR HARDIE ON KING GEORGE V

•

For seventeen years, he did nothing at all but
kill animals and stick in stamps.
— HAROLD NICOLSON ON KING GEORGE V

•

His intellect is of no more use than a pistol packed in the bottom of a
trunk in the robber-infested Apennines.
— PRINCE ALBERT ON HIS SON EDWARD, PRINCE OF WALES,
LATER KING EDWARD VII

A pimple on the arse of the Empire.

—COUNT ALFRED DE MARIGNY, REFERRING TO THE DUKE OF
WINDSOR, FORMERLY KING EDWARD VIII

I'm prepared to take advice on leisure from Prince Philip. He's a world
expert on leisure. He's been practicing most of his adult life.

—NEIL KINNOCK ON PRINCE PHILIP, DUKE OF EDINBURGH

And Royalty Elsewhere:

What can you do with a man who looks like a
female llama surprised when bathing?

—SIR WINSTON CHURCHILL ON CHARLES DE GAULLE

. . . an angry, evil and embittered little bishop

—ZIMBABWE PRESIDENT ROBERT MUGABE ON
SOUTH AFRICAN ARCHBISHOP DESMOND TUTU

And the devil came here yesterday. Yesterday the devil came here.
Right here. And it smells of sulphur still today.
—VENEZUELAN PRESIDENT HUGO CHAVEZ
REFERRING TO PRESIDENT GEORGE W. BUSH'S
APPEARANCE AT THE UNITED NATIONS

I know that in Italy there is a man producing a film on Nazi
concentration camps—I shall put you forward for the role of Kapo
(guard chosen from among the prisoners)—you would be perfect.
—ITALIAN PRIME MINISTER SILVIO BERLUSCONI TO GERMAN
MEMBER OF THE EUROPEAN PARLIAMENT MARTIN SCHULZ

[He clings] to data the way a drunkard clings to lampposts.
—ITALIAN POLITICIAN PAOLO ROMANI ON SILVIO BERLUSCONI

Don't be so humble, you're not that great.
— ISRAEL'S PRIME MINISTER GOLDA MEIR TO GENERAL MOSHE
DAYAN

. . . the son of 60,000 whores
— SYRIAN DEFENSE MINISTER GENERAL MUSTAFA TLASS ON
PALESTINE AUTHORITY LEADER YASSER ARAFAT

. . . the charisma of a damp rag [and a] low-grade bank clerk
— NIGEL FARAGE, LEADER OF BRITAIN'S
INDEPENDENCE PARTY, ON EUROPEAN
COUNCIL PRESIDENT HERMAN VAN ROMPUY

The Leader of the Opposition is more to be pitied than despised, the poor old thing. The Liberal Party of Australia ought to put him down like a faithful old dog because he is of no use to it and of no use to the nation.
—AUSTRALIAN PRIME MINISTER PAUL KEATING ON OPPOSITION LEADER ANDREW PEACOCK

•

He's wound up like a thousand-day clock! One (more half) turn and there'll be springs and sprockets all over the building. Mr. Speaker, give him a Valium.
—PAUL KEATING TO OPPOSITION LEADER JOHN HOWARD

•

He's like a shiver waiting for a spine.
—PAUL KEATING ON MEMBER OF AUSTRALIAN PARLIAMENT JOHN HEWSON

•

You boxhead, you wouldn't know. You are flat out counting past ten. You stupid, foul-mouthed grub.
—PAUL KEATING ON SHADOW MINISTER WILSON TUCKEY

Chapter

· · · · · · · · · · · ·

III

Lean and Mean: One-Line Quips

While you remain at home your hair is at the hairdresser's; you take out your teeth at night and sleep tucked away in a hundred cosmetics boxes—even your face does not sleep with you.
—MARTIAL (MARCUS VALERIUS MARTIALIS),
TO AN UNNAMED WOMAN

I have more talent in my smallest fart than
you have in your entire body.
—ACTOR WALTER MATTHAU TO BARBRA STREISAND

. . . a solemn, unsmiling, sanctimonious old iceberg who looked like he was waiting for a vacancy in the Trinity.
—MARK TWAIN, OF A FELLOW PASSENGER TO THE HOLY LAND

I see her as one great stampede of lips directed at the nearest derriere.
—NOEL COWARD ON AN UNNAMED ACTRESS

Hah! I always knew Frank would end up in bed with a boy!
—AVA GARDNER ON MIA FARROW'S
MARRIAGE TO FRANK SINATRA

His face was filled with broken commandments.
—JOHN MASEFIELD ON AN UNNAMED MAN

He looks like he's walking around just to save funeral expenses.
—JOHN HUSTON ON ACTOR PETER O'TOOLE

She has a face that belongs to the sea and the wind, with large rocking-horse nostrils and teeth that you just know bite an apple every day.
—CECIL BEATON ON KATHARINE HEPBURN

I just think he and Microsoft are a bit narrow. He'd be a broader guy if he had dropped acid once or gone off to an ashram when he was younger.
—STEVE JOBS ON BILL GATES

. . . a rather woebegone cocker spaniel . . .
—MOSS HART ON MEL FERRER

Last week, I stated this woman was the ugliest woman I had ever seen.
I have since been visited by her sister, and now wish to withdraw
that statement.
—**MARK TWAIN**

The Duchess of Dowdy
—**MR. BLACKWELL ON CAMILLA, DUCHESS OF CORNWALL**

The only genius with an IQ of 6.
—**GORE VIDAL ON ANDY WARHOL**

She runs the gamut of emotions from A to B.
—**DOROTHY PARKER ON KATHARINE HEPBURN**

No woman of our time has gone further with less mental equipment.
—CLIFTON FADIMAN ON AUTHOR, CONGRESSWOMAN,
AND AMBASSADOR CLARE BOOTH LUCE

She looked like a huge ball of fur on two well-developed legs.
—NANCY MITFORD ON PRINCESS MARGARET

Joan Rivers's face hasn't just had a lift, it's taken the elevator all the
way to the top floor without stopping.
—CLIVE JAMES

She was so ugly she could make a mule back away from an oat bin.
—WILL ROGERS

She was what we used to call a suicide blonde—dyed by her own hand.
—SAUL BELLOW

He had a winning smile, but everything else was a loser.
—GEORGE C. SCOTT ON WALTER KERR

She's about as feminine as a sidewalk drill.
—MARYON ALLEN ON PHYLLIS SCHLAFLY

In his body-building days Arnold Schwarzenegger was
know as the Austrian Oak. Then he started acting and
was known as . . . the Austrian Oak.
—REALITY TELEVISION PERSONALITY JACKIE DEE

I feel so miserable without you, it's almost like having you here.
—SINGER-SONGWRITER STEPHEN BISHOP

This is one Hilton that should be closed for renovation.
—MR. BLACKWELL ON PARIS HILTON

You've heard of people living in a fool's paradise? . . . well,
Leonora [Corbett] has a duplex there.
—GEORGE S. KAUFMAN

You're a parasite for sore eyes.
—GREGORY RATOFF

Sometimes I need what only you can provide: your absence.
—CARTOONIST ASHLEIGH BRILLIANT

There's nothing wrong with you that reincarnation won't cure.
—COMEDIAN JACK E. LEONARD

You had to stand in line to hate him.
—HEDDA HOPPER ON HOLLYWOOD STUDIO HEAD HARRY COHN

I'll bet your father spent the first year of your life
throwing rocks at the stork.
—SCREENWRITER IRVING BRECHER

He is an old bore. Even the grave yawns for him.
—ACTOR HERBERT BEERBOHM TREE

You're a good example of why some animals eat their young.
—JIM SAMUELS

Do you want to spend the rest of your life selling sugared water or do
you want a chance to change the world?
—STEVE JOBS TO JOHN SCULLEY, PRESIDENT OF PEPSI COLA

I've just learned about his illness. Let's hope it's nothing trivial.
—IRVIN S. COBB

If you ever become a mother, can I have one of the puppies?
—WRITER CHARLES PIERCE

•

He knows so little and knows it so fluently.
—ELLEN GLASGOW

•

Pushing forty? She's hanging on for dear life.
—DAME IVY COMPTON-BURNETT

•

About the only thing you can say for his constipation
of ideas is his diarrhea of words.
—GEORGE JEAN NATHAN

You have a good and kind soul. It just doesn't match the rest of you.
—RESEARCH PROGRAMMER NORM PAPERNICK

You take the lies out of him, and he'll shrink to the size of your hat;
you take the malice out of him, and he'll disappear.
—SAMUEL L. CLEMONS (MARK TWAIN)

I never liked him and I always will.
—BRITISH POP SINGER DAVE CLARK

I like long walks, especially when they are taken by people who
annoy me.
—FRED ALLEN

I regard you with an indifference bordering on aversion.
—ROBERT LOUIS STEVENSON

His ears made him look like a taxicab with both doors open.
—HOWARD HUGHES ON ACTOR CLARK GABLE

The more I think of you, the less I think of you.
—HENNY YOUNGMAN

He's completely unspoiled by failure.
—NOEL COWARD

When I can't sleep, I read a book by Steve Allen.
—OSCAR LEVANT

Sir, your wife, under pretense of keeping a bawdy-house,

is a receiver of stolen goods.

—SAMUEL JOHNSON

His mother should have thrown him away and kept the stork.

—MAE WEST

She wears her clothes as if they were thrown on with a pitch folk.

—JONATHAN SWIFT

I could never learn to like her, except on a raft at

sea with no other provisions in sight.

—SAMUEL L. CLEMONS (MARK TWAIN)

Every time I look at you I get a fierce desire to be lonesome.
—OSCAR LEVANT

No one can have a higher opinion of him than I have;
and I think he's a dirty little beast.
—W. S. GILBERT, LYRICIST PARTNER OF COMPOSER
ARTHUR SULLIVAN AS GILBERT & SULLIVAN

You're a mouse studying to be a rat.
—WILSON MIZNER

I see the pain on your face when you say the word intellectual,
because it has so many syllables in it.
—CLIVE JAMES

Overhyped and underdressed, what's happened to Lindsay? When it comes to fashion, she's in a schizophrenic frenzy!
— MR. BLACKWELL ON ACTRESS LINDSAY LOHAN

The perfection of rottenness.
— WILLIAM JAMES

He was so narrow-minded that if he fell on a pin it would blind him in both eyes.
— FRED ALLEN

It's a new low for actresses when you have to wonder what's between her ears instead of her legs.
— KATHARINE HEPBURN ABOUT SHARON STONE

He was distinguished for ignorance; for he had only

one idea and that was wrong.

—BENJAMIN DISRAELI

When I see a man of shallow understanding extravagantly clothed,

I feel sorry—for the clothes.

—JOSH BILLINGS

You've baked a really lovely cake, but then you've

used dog shit for frosting.

—STEVE JOBS TO A DESIGNER AT APPLE

. . . Shrink-wrapped cheesecake.

—MR. BLACKWELL ON MARIAH CAREY

Michael Jackson was a poor black boy who grew up
to be a rich white woman.
— **MOLLY IVINS**

Look, let me put it to you this way: The NFL all too often looks like a
game between the Bloods and the Crips without any weapons.
— **RUSH LIMBAUGH**

Why do you sit there looking like an envelope
without any address on it?
— **MARK TWAIN**

Why don't you get a haircut? You look like a chrysanthemum.
— **P. G. WODEHOUSE**

You couldn't tell if she was dressed for an opera or an operation.

—IRVIN S. COBB

. . . A brain of feathers, and a heart of lead

—ALEXANDER POPE

Ricardo Montalban is to improvisational acting what
Mount Rushmore is to animation.

—JOHN CASSAVETES

. . . A mental midget with the IQ of a fence post

—TOM WAITS

. . . A wit with dunces, and a dunce with wits.
—**ALEXANDER POPE**

. . . Doesn't know much, but leads the league in nostril hair.
—**JOSH BILLINGS**

Where does she find them?
—**DOROTHY PARKER, ON BEING TOLD THAT CLARE
BOOTHE LUCE WAS KIND TO HER INFERIORS**

He has the attention span of a lightning bolt.
—**ACTOR ROBERT REDFORD**

An editor should have a pimp for a brother so
he'd have someone to look up to.
—GENE FOWLER

Stay with me; I want to be alone.
—JOEY ADAMS

I've just spent an hour talking to Tallulah for a few minutes.
—ACTOR FRED KEATING ON ACTRESS TALLULAH BANKHEAD

That young girl is one of the least benightedly unintelligent
organic life forms it has been my profound lack of pleasure
not to be able to avoid meeting.
—DOUGLAS ADAMS

He's so small, he's a waste of skin.

—FRED ALLEN

•

If you had your life to live over again, do it overseas.

—HENNY YOUNGMAN

•

. . . Useless as a pulled tooth

—MARY ROBERTS RINEHART

•

She's a global fashion curse.

—MR. BLACKWELL ON JESSICA SIMPSON

•

She has discovered the secret of perpetual middle age.

—OSCAR LEVANT ON ACTRESS ZSA ZSA GABOR

While he was not dumber than an ox, he was not any smarter either.
—JAMES THURBER

Barbara Walters is said to sleep standing so
that the silicone won't move.
—JOURNALIST AND WRITER TAKI

They say you shouldn't say nothin' about the dead unless
it's good. He's dead. Good.
—COMEDIAN MOMS MABLEY

Why am I so good at playing bitches? I think it's because I'm not a
bitch; maybe that's why Miss Crawford always plays ladies.
—BETTE DAVIS ON ACTRESS JOAN CRAWFORD

He's got a wonderful head for money. There's this long slit on the top.
—SIR DAVID FROST

He couldn't mastermind an electric bulb into a socket.
—ACTRESS FANNY BRICE ON HUSBAND NICKY ARNSTEIN

I remember the time I was kidnapped and they sent a piece of my finger to my father. He said he wanted more proof.
—RODNEY DANGERFIELD

No, no; the "t" is silent, as in "Harlow."
—MARGOT ASQUITH CORRECTING ACTRESS JEAN HARLOW'S MISPRONUNCIATION OF "MARGOT"

Maybe it's the hair, maybe it's the teeth,

maybe it's the intellect . . . no, it's the hair.

—TOM SHALES ON ACTRESS FARRAH FAWCETT-MAJORS

•

When you use your brain it's a violation of the child labor law.

—COMEDIAN JOE E. LEWIS

•

He's a self-made man . . . the living proof of the horrors of

unskilled labor!

—ACTOR ED WYNN

•

What's on your mind?—if you'll forgive the overstatement.

—FRED ALLEN

. . . About as cuddly as a cornered ferret.
—JOURNALIST LYNN BARBER ON TV PERSONALITY
ANNE ROBINSON

His ignorance covers the world like a blanket, and
there's scarcely a hole in it anywhere.
—MARK TWAIN

What do you mean, heart attack? . . . You've got
to have a heart before you can have an attack.
—BILLY WILDER ON ACTOR PETER SELLERS

She's the sort of woman who lives for others—you
can tell the others by their hunted expression.
—C. S. LEWIS

It proves what Harry always said: Give the public
what they want and they'll come out for it.
**—RED SKELTON ON HOLLYWOOD MOGUL
HARRY COHN'S WELL-ATTENDED FUNERAL**

. . . So boring you fall asleep halfway through her name.
—BRITISH PLAYWRIGHT AND AUTHOR ALAN BENNETT

She looks like a masculine Bride of Frankenstein.
—MR. BLACKWELL ON BARBRA STREISAND

I've just learned about his illness; let's hope it's nothing trivial.
—IRVIN S. COBB

She never lets ideas interrupt the easy flow of her conversation.
—AUTHOR JEAN WEBSTER

•

She is a peacock in everything but beauty.
—OSCAR WILDE

•

She has been kissed as often as a police-court Bible,
and by much the same class of people.
—ROBERTSON DAVIES

•

Louis B. Mayer's arm around your shoulder meant
his hand was closer to your throat.
—JULES DASSIN

There goes the original good time that's been had by all.
—LEONORA CORBETT ON AN UNNAMED ACTRESS

●

She is such a good friend that she would throw all her acquaintances
into the water for the pleasure of fishing them out again.
—CHARLES-MAURICE DE TALLEYRAND-PERIGORD

●

She tells enough white lies to ice a wedding cake.
—MARGOT ASQUITH

●

The Bare-Bottomed Bore of Babylon
—MR. BLACKWELL ON MADONNA

●

She should get a divorce and settle down.
—JACK PAAR ON ELIZABETH TAYLOR

She not only worships the golden calf, she barbecues it for lunch.
—OSCAR LEVANT ON ZSA ZSA GABOR

•

I'd call him a sadistic, hippophilic necrophile,
but that would be beating a dead horse.
—WOODY ALLEN

And a Sprinkling of Classic Insults:

—I had a nightmare. I dreamt I was you.

•

—You look like you fell out of the ugly tree and
hit every branch on the way down.

•

—What's that ugly thing growing out of your neck . . . oh,
sorry—it's your head.

— Shouldn't you have a license for being that ugly?

—Folks clap when they see you . . . but they clap their hands over their eyes.

—You've got the perfect weapon against muggers—your face.

—Frankenstein called—he wants his face back.

—Somebody woke up on the wrong side of the cage this morning.

—Calling you an idiot would be an insult to other idiots.

—I heard that you went to a haunted house and were offered a job.

—Why don't you slip into something comfortable—like a coma.

—Since opposites attract, you'll fall for somebody who's attractive, honest, intelligent, and cultured.

—Don't let your mind wander. It's way too small to be outside by itself.

—Everyone is entitled to be stupid, but you abuse the privilege.

—How many times did your parents drop you when you were a baby?

—Why don't you just open your mind and shut your mouth?
Both are empty anyway.

—Keep talking; someday you might say something intelligent.

—Come again when you can't stay so long.

—I'd like to give you a going-away present . . . but
you have to do your part.

—Any similarity between you and a human is purely coincidental.

—Are you always so stupid or is today a special occasion?

—As an outsider, what do you think of the human race?

—I'd kick you in the teeth, but why should I improve your looks?

—At least there's one thing good about your body.
It isn't as ugly as your face.

—Brains aren't everything. In fact, in your case they're nothing.

—People say I've no taste, but I like you anyway . . . or maybe not.

—Did your parents pay you to run away from home?

—With a face like yours, you should sue your parents.

—Are you devoting your life to spreading ignorance?

—If laughter is the best medicine, your face must be curing the world.

—You have your entire life to be a jerk. Why not take today off?

—Your ass must be pretty jealous of all the shit that comes out of your mouth.

—Remember when I asked for your opinion? Me neither.

—If you're waiting for me to care, I hope you brought something to eat, 'cause it's gonna be a really long time.

•

—Some day you'll go far—and I really hope you stay there. I'm trying my absolute hardest to see things from your perspective, but I just can't get my head that far up my ass.

•

—You have a brow unfurrowed by care or thought.

•

— Don't think; it may sprain your brain.

•

—You must have been born on a highway because that's where most accidents happen.

—People like you don't grow on trees—they swing from trees.

—You have a mechanical mind. Too bad
you forgot to wind it this morning.

—Your steel-trap mind is always closed.

—No wonder you're always lost in thought—it's unfamiliar territory.

—You're dark and handsome. When it's dark, you're handsome.

—Your ideas are miraculous. If you have an idea, it's a miracle.

—Are you listed in *Who's Who,* or in *What's That?*

—Scientists would use you as a blueprint to build an idiot.

—Why are you here? Isn't the zoo is closed at night?

—When you were born, your mother said, "Aw, what a treasure," and your father said "Yeah, let's bury it."

—How much refund do you expect on your head now that it's empty?

—How would you like to feel the way you look?

—I can't talk to you right now; where will you be ten years from now?

—Don't turn the other cheek—it's just as ugly.

—You shouldn't play hide and seek—no one would look for you.

—Keep taking whatever you take to be so stupid—it really works.

—I could make a monkey out of you,
but why should I take all the credit?

—I can't seem to remember your name, but please don't help me.

—You say you're a self-made man. It's nice of you to take the blame!

—I'm not saying I hate you, but I would unplug your
life support to charge my phone.

—You're not as stupid as you look. Nobody could be.

Snappy Comebacks to Pick-Up Lines:

"Haven't we met before?"
"Yes, I'm the receptionist at the VD clinic."

"Haven't I seen you someplace before?"
"Yeah, that's why I don't go there anymore."

"Is this seat empty?"

"Yes, and mine will be too if you sit down."

•

"So, wanna go back to my place?"

"Well, I don't know. Will two people fit under a rock?"

•

"Your place or mine?"

"Both. You go to yours and I'll go to mine."

•

"I'd like to call you. What's your number?"

"It's in the phone book."

"But I don't know your name."

"That's in the phone book too."

•

"What sign were you born under?"

"No Parking."

"Hey, baby, what's your sign?"

"Do Not Enter."

•

"How do you like your eggs in the morning?"

"Unfertilized!"

•

"I know how to please a woman."

"Then please leave me alone."

•

"I want to give myself to you."

"Sorry, I don't accept cheap gifts."

•

"I can tell that you want me."

"Ohhhh. You're so right. I want you to leave."

"If I could see you naked, I'd die happy."

"Yeah, but if I saw you naked, I'd probably die laughing."

"Your body is like a temple."

"Sorry, there are no services today."

"I'd go through anything for you."

"Good! Let's start with your bank account."

"I would go to the end of the world for you."

"Yes, but would you stay there?"

Snappy Comebacks for a Patient in the Hospital:

"And how are we this morning?"

"Judging by the way I feel and the way you look,

I'd say we're both in trouble."

"I know someone who had the very same thing
last year, and today he's fine!"
"That was me—and I got it again."

•

"We'll have you up and around before you know it."
"And probably before I'm ready."

•

"I just dropped by! I can only stay a minute."
"I'll start the timer now."

•

"If there's anything you want, don't hesitate to ask."
"OK—shut the door from the outside."

Chapter

· · · · · · · · · · ·

IV

Running Down America:
Bad-Mouthing the USA

States:

- Arkansas fire extinguisher: a chamber pot

- Arkansas toothpick: a knife with a long blade

- Arkansas travels: diarrhea

- Boston (Massachusetts) screwdriver: a hammer, used to hammer in a screw

California is a fine place to live . . . if you happen to be an orange.
—FRED ALLEN

* Cape Cod (Massachusetts) turkey: codfish

* Georgia bacon: meat from a gopher tortoise

* Hawaiian time: a disregard for punctuality

* Kentucky breakfast: a bottle of bourbon

- Kentucky pill: a bullet

- Maniac: a resident of Maine

- Masshole: New Hampshire term for someone
who moved there from Massachusetts

- Ohio shower: disinfectant toilet wipes

If I owned Texas and Hell, I would rent out Texas and live in Hell.
—CIVIL WAR GENERAL PHILIP H. SHERIDAN

• Virginia caviar: black-eyed peas

American Cities:

Here is the difference between Dante, Milton, and me. They wrote
about Hell and never saw the place. I wrote about Chicago after
looking the town over for years and years.
—CARL SANDBURG

•

Hollywood is a sewer with service from the Ritz.
—WILSON MIZNER

•

Las Vegas: Spanish for "lost wages."
—SOURCE UNKNOWN

New York is a city of seven million so decadent that when I leave it I never dare look back lest I turn into salt and the conductor throw me over his left shoulder for good luck.

—JOURNALIST FRANK SULLIVAN

•

I prefer a wet San Francisco to a dry Manhattan.

—SOURCE UNKNOWN

•

Speaking of New York, as a traveller I have two faults to find with it. In the first place there is nothing to see; and in the second place there is no mode of getting about to see anything.

—ANTHONY TROLLOPE

As many of you know, I came from San Francisco. We don't have a lot of farms there. Well, we do have one—it's a mushroom farm, so you know what that means.
— POLITICIAN NANCY PELOSI

And for the United States in Its Entirety. . .

I am willing to love all mankind, except an American.
— SAMUEL JOHNSON

America is one long expectoration.
— OSCAR WILDE

The American has no language, he has a dialect, slang, provincialism, accent and so forth.
— RUDYARD KIPLING

America is the only nation in history which has miraculously
gone directly from barbarism to degeneration without
the usual interval of civilization.
—GEORGES CLEMENCEAU

If you're going to America, bring your own food.
—AUTHOR FRAN LEBOWITZ

When you become used to never being alone, you may consider
yourself Americanised.
—ANDRÉ MAUROIS

No one ever went broke underestimating the
taste of the American public.
—H. L. MENCKEN

It was wonderful to find America, but perhaps it would have been more
wonderful to miss it.
—SAMUEL L. CLEMONS

There is nothing the matter with Americans except their ideals. The
real American is all right; it is the ideal American who is all wrong.
—G. K. CHESTERTON

[Americans'] demeanour is invariably morose, sullen, clownish and repulsive. I should think there is not, on the face of the earth, a people so entirely destitute of humour, vivacity, or the capacity of enjoyment.
—CHARLES DICKENS

The American nation in the sixth ward is a fine people; they love the eagle—on the back of a dollar.
—HUMORIST AND AUTHOR FINLAY PETER DUNNE

No one can be as calculatedly rude as the British, which amazes Americans, who do not understand studied insult and can only offer abuse as a substitute.
—NOVELIST PAUL GALLICO

Knavery seems to be so much the striking feature of [America's] inhabitants that it may not in the end be an evil that they will become aliens to this country.
—KING GEORGE III

The organization of American society is an interlocking system of semi-monopolies notoriously venal, an electorate notoriously unenlightened, misled by a mass media notoriously phony.
—WRITER PAUL GOODMAN

Sir, [Americans] are a race of convicts and ought to be grateful for anything we allow them short of hanging.
—SAMUEL JOHNSON

Americans are people who laugh at African witch doctors and spend one-hundred million dollars on fake reducing systems.
—JOURNALIST L. L. LEVINSON

There won't be any revolution in America . . . the people are too clean. They spend all their time changing their shirts and washing themselves. You can't feel fierce and revolutionary in a bathroom.
—ERIC LINKLATER

The trouble with America is that there are far too many wide open spaces surrounded by teeth.
—BUSINESSMAN AND ARCHITECT CHARLES LUCKMAN

The American political system is like fast food—mushy, insipid, made

out of disgusting parts of things and everybody wants some.

—**P. J. O'ROURKE**

The national dish of America is menus.

—**ARCHITECT ROBERT ROBINSON**

Frustrate a Frenchman, he will drink himself to death; an Irishman,

he will die of angry hypertension; a Dane, he will shoot himself; an

American, he will get drunk, shoot you, then establish a million-dollar

aid programme for your relatives. Then he will die of an ulcer.

—**AUTHOR S. A. RUDIN**

America . . . where laws and customs alike are
based on the dreams of spinsters.
—BERTRAND RUSSELL

The 100-percent American is 99-percent idiot.
—GEORGE BERNARD SHAW

The American male doesn't mature until he has exhausted all
other possibilities.
—WILFRED SHEED

In the four corners of the globe, who reads an American book? or goes to an American play? or looks at an American picture or statue? What does the world yet owe to America's physicians and surgeons? . . . Who drinks out of American glasses? or eats from American plates? or wears American coats and gowns? or sleeps in American blankets? Finally, under which of the old tyrannical governments of Europe is every sixth man a slave, whom his fellow creatures may buy and sell and torture?
—**REVEREND SYDNEY SMITH**

I found there a country with thirty-two religions and only one sauce.
—**CHARLES-MAURICE DE TALLEYRAND-PERIGORD**

America . . . just a nation of two-hundred-million used car salesmen with all the money we need to buy guns and no qualms about killing anybody else in the world who tries to make us uncomfortable.
—**HUNTER S. THOMPSON**

America is a large, friendly dog in a very small room. Every time it
wags its tail it knocks over a chair.
—ARNOLD TOYNBEE

•

I heard an Englishman, who had been long resident in America,
declare that in following, in meeting, or in overtaking, in the street, on
the road, or in the field, at the theatre, the coffee-house, or at home,
he had never overheard Americans conversing without the word
DOLLAR being pronounced between them. Such unity of purpose . . .
can . . . be found nowhere else, except . . . in an ant's nest.
—ENGLISH AUTHOR AND TRAVELLER FRANCES TROLLOPE

•

It is by the goodness of God that in our country we have those three
unspeakably precious things: freedom of speech, freedom of conscience,
and the prudence never to practice either of them.
—SAMUEL L. CLEMONS (MARK TWAIN)

The hatred Americans have for their own government is pathological . . . at one level it is simply thwarted greed: since our religion is making a buck, giving a part of that buck to any government is an act against nature.
— GORE VIDAL

The Americans, like the English, probably make love worse than any other race.
— WALT WHITMAN

In America everybody is of the opinion that he has no social superiors, since all men are equal, but he does not admit that he has no social inferiors.
— BERTRAND RUSSELL

When good Americans die, they go to Paris; when bad Americans die, they go to America.
— OSCAR WILDE

Chapter
. . . .
V

Country Rudes: International Insults

Canada could have had French culture, American know-how, and English government. Instead it got French government, English know-how, and American culture.
—VIDEO DIRECTOR JOHN COLOMBO

This gloomy [Canadian] region, where the year is divided into one day and one night, lies entirely outside the stream of history.
—W. W. READE

I don't even know what street Canada is on.
—AL CAPONE

Canada is a country so square that even the female impersonators are women.
—COMEDIAN RICHARD BRENNER

It makes little difference, Canada is useful only to provide me with furs.
—MADAME DE POMPADOUR

I fear that I have not got much to say about Canada, not having seen much; what I got by going to Canada was a cold.
—HENRY DAVID THOREAU

You know that these two nations [Britain and France] are at war for a few acres of snow, and they are spending . . . more than all of Canada is worth.
—VOLTAIRE

. . . A subarctic lumber village converted by Royal Mandate into a political cock-fighting pit.
—GOLDWIN SMITH ON OTTAWA

I find that Newfoundland is said to be celebrated for its codfish, its dogs, its hogs and its fogs.

—PREMIER OF NEWFOUNDLAND SIR WILLIAM WHITEWAY

•

The purity of the air of Newfoundland is without doubt due to the fact that the people never open their windows.

—BRITISH ARTIST, NATURALIST, AND WRITER J. G. MILLAIS

•

Montreal is the only place where a good French accent isn't a social asset.

—BRENDAN BEHAN

•

Toronto as a city carries out the idea of Canada as a country. It is a calculated crime both against the aspirations of the soul and the affection of the heart.

—ENGLISH POET AND PAINTER ALEISTER CROWLEY

Curse the blasted, jelly-boned swines, the slimy, the belly-wriggling invertebrates, the miserable soddingrotters, the flaming sods, the sniveling, dribbling, dithering, palsied, pulse-less lot that make up England today. They've got white of egg in their veins, and their spunk is that watery it's a marvel they can breed.

—D. H. LAWRENCE

. . . Unmitigated noodles

—KAISER WILHELM II ON ENGLAND

A demon took a monkey to wife—the results, by the grace of God, was the English.

—INDIAN SAYING

I know why the sun never sets on the British Empire: God wouldn't trust an Englishman in the dark.

—PRINCETON PROFESSOR DUNCAN SPAETH

English coffee tastes like water that has been
squeezed out of a wet sleeve.
—FRED ALLEN

•

The English think soap is civilization.
—GERMAN HISTORIAN AND POLITICIAN HEINRICH VON
TREITSCHKE

•

Continental people have a sex life; the English have hot-water bottles.
—AUTHOR GEORGE MIKES

•

Paralytic sycophants, effete betrayers of humanity, carrion-eating
servile imitators, arch-cowards and collaborators, gang of women-
murderers, degenerate rabble, parasitic traditionalists, playboy
soldiers, conceited dandies.
—COMMUNIST EAST GERMAN PROPAGANDA
DESCRIPTION OF THE BRITISH

The Englishman who has lost his fortune is said

to have died of a broken heart.

—**RALPH WALDO EMERSON**

•

Britain is the only country in the world where the

food is more dangerous than the sex.

—**COMEDIAN JACKIE MASON**

•

If you live in Birmingham [England], then being awake is not

necessarily a desirable state.

—**POP MUSIC PRODUCER AND JOURNALIST TONY WILSON**

•

When it's three o'clock in New York, it's still 1938 in London.

—**BETTE MIDLER**

The way to endure summer in England is to have it
framed and glazed in a comfortable room.
—**HORACE WALPOLE**

•

The English country gentleman galloping after a fox—the
unspeakable in full pursuit of the uneatable.
—**OSCAR WILDE**

•

England, the heart of a rabbit in the body of a lion. The jaws of a
serpent, in an abode of popinjays.
—**ARTIST EUGENE DESCHAMPS**

•

If one could teach the English to talk and the Irish to listen,
society would be quite civilised.
—**OSCAR WILDE**

Give an Irishman lager for a month, and he's a dead man. An Irishman is lined with copper, and the beer corrodes it, but whiskey polishes the copper and is the saving of him.

—MARK TWAIN

•

Put an Irishman on a spit and you can always find another one to turn him.

—GEORGE BERNARD SHAW

•

Other people have a nationality. The Irish and the Jews have a psychosis.

—BRENDAN BEHAN

•

As sluttish and slatternly as an Irishwoman bred in France.

—IRISH SAYING

Ireland is the sow that eats her farrow.
—JAMES JOYCE

The Irish are a fair people, they never speak well of one another.
—SAMUEL JOHNSON

Like an Irishman's obligation, all on the one side, and always yours.
—ENGLISH SAYING

For the Irish, there are no stars in the sky.
—ENGLISH SAYING

This is one race of people for whom psychoanalysis
is of no use whatsoever.
—SIGMUND FREUD ON THE IRISH

The trouble with Ireland is that it's a country full of genius,
with absolutely no talent.
—HUGH LEONARD

•

I have been trying all my life to like Scotchmen, and am obligated to
desist from the experiment in despair.
—CHARLES LAMB

•

The noblest prospect which a Scotchman ever sees, is the
high road that leads him to England.
—SAMUEL JOHNSON

•

Scotland: That garret of the earth—that knuckle-end of England—
that land of Calvin, oatcakes, and sulfur.
—REVEREND SYDNEY SMITH

Asked by a Scot what Johnson thought of Scotland: "That it is a very vile country, to be sure, Sir."

"Well, Sir! (replies the Scot, somewhat mortified), God made it."

Johnson: "Certainly he did; but we must always remember that he made it for Scotchmen, and comparisons are odious, Mr. S———; but God made hell."

—JAMES BOSWELL, IN HIS *LIFE OF SAMUEL JOHNSON*

Scotland: A land of meanness, sophistry and lust.

—LORD BYRON

It requires a surgical operation to get a joke well into a Scotsman's understanding.

—REVEREND SYDNEY SMITH

The great thing about Glasgow now is that if there is a nuclear attack it'll look exactly the same afterwards.

—ACTOR AND COMEDIAN BILLY CONNOLLY

[Wales is] the land of my fathers, and my fathers can have it.

—DYLAN THOMAS

There are still parts of Wales where the only

concession to gaiety is a striped shroud.

—WELSH WRITER AND BROADCASTER GWYN THOMAS

He who would eat in Spain must bring his kitchen along.

—GERMAN SAYING

The Spaniard is a bad servant, but a worse master.

—ENGLISH SAYING

A Spaniard may be trusted, but no further than your nose.

—GERMAN SAYING

The only good thing that comes from the east is the sun.

—PORTUGUESE SAYING

•

Take from a Spaniard all his good qualities,

and there remains a Portuguese.

—SPANISH SAYING

•

The friendship of the French is like their wine,

exquisite, but of short duration.

—GERMAN SAYING

•

If the French were really intelligent, they'd speak English.

—WILFRED SHEED

France is a dog hole, and it no more merits the tread of a man's foot.
—**WILLIAM SHAKESPEARE, IN** *ALL'S WELL THAT END'S WELL*

It took no more effort than casting a Frenchman into Hell.
—**DUTCH SAYING**

France is a country where the money falls apart in your hands
and you can't tear the toilet paper.
—**BILLY WILDER**

The French are sawed-off sissies who eat snails and slugs and cheese
that smells like people's feet. Utter cowards who force their own
children to drink wine, they gibber like baboons even when you
try to speak to them in their own wimpy language.
—**P. J. O'ROURKE**

Paris is like a whore. From a distance she seems ravishing, you can't wait until you have her in your arms. Five minutes later you feel empty, disgusted with yourself. You feel tricked.

—HENRY MILLER

•

A fighting Frenchman runs away from even a she-goat.

—RUSSIAN SAYING

•

I do not dislike the French from the vulgar antipathy between neighboring nations, but for their insolent and unfounded airs of superiority.

—HORACE WALPOLE

•

The German may be a good fellow, but it is best to hang him just the same.

—RUSSIAN SAYING

Germany, the diseased world's bathhouse.
— **MARK TWAIN**

One thing I will say about the Germans, they are always perfectly

willing to give somebody's land to somebody else.
— **WILL ROGERS**

Marry a German and you'll see that the women have hairy tongues.
— **ROMANIAN SAYING**

I speak Spanish to God, Italian to women, French to men,

and German to my horse.
— **EMPEROR CHARLES V OF THE HOLY ROMAN EMPIRE**

German is a language which was developed solely to afford the speaker the opportunity to spit at strangers under the guise of polite conversation.

—*NATIONAL LAMPOON*

•

Because of their cuisine, Germans don't consider farting rude. They'd certainly be out of luck if they did.

—P. J. O'ROURKE

•

German is the most extravagantly ugly language—it sounds like someone using a sick bag on a 747.

—WILLIE RUSHTON

•

The German mind has a talent for making no mistakes but the very greatest.

—CLIFTON FADIMAN

You can always reason with a German. You can always reason with a

barnyard animal, too, for all the good it does.

—P. J. O'ROURKE

The Germans are like women. You can scarcely ever fathom their

depths—they haven't any.

—FRIEDRICH WILHELM NIETZSCHE

If there is a Hell, Rome is built on top of it.

—GERMAN SAYING

Rome reminds me of a man who lives by exhibiting

to travelers his grandmother's corpse.

—JAMES JOYCE

Half an Italian in a house is one too many.
— GERMAN SAYING

•

Germans are flummoxed by humor, the Swiss have no concept of fun,
the Spanish think there is nothing at all ridiculous about eating dinner
at midnight, and the Italians should never, ever have been let in on
the invention of the motor car.
— BILL BRYSON

•

There are two Italies . . . The one is the most sublime and lovely
contemplation that can be conceived by the imagination of man; the
other is the most degraded, disgusting, and odious. What do you think?
Young women of rank actually eat—you will never guess what—
garlick! Our poor friend Lord Byron is quite corrupted by living among
these people, and in fact, is going on in a way not worthy of him.
— PERCY BYSSHE SHELLEY

Italian soup.
—CZECH EXPRESSION FOR POISON

To cook an egg, to make a bed for a dog, and to teach an Italian to do
anything are three hard things.
—GERMAN SAYING

The Italian will kill his father for money.
—GREEK SAYING

Q: How many Italians does it take to screw in a light bulb?
A: Two. One to screw it in, and the other to shoot the witness.
—WIDESPREAD JOKE

Cross yourself once before an Andalusian and
thrice on spotting an Italian.
—SPANISH SAYING

There are few virtues which the Poles do not possess and
there are few errors they have ever avoided.
—SIR WINSTON CHURCHILL

•

Why does the devil take the Poles? Because they are glad to go along.
—RUSSIAN SAYING

•

A country to be in for two hours, to two-and-a-half hours, if the
weather is fine, and no more. Ennui comes in the third hour and
suicide attacks you before the night.
—LORD CHANCELLOR LORD BROUGHAM ON SWITZERLAND

•

Did hogs feed here or did Lithuanians have a feast here?
—POLISH SAYING

•

How can you tell a Russian? Go to sleep and he will rob you.
—UKRAINIAN SAYING

In Russia a man is called reactionary if he objects to having his property stolen and his wife and children murdered.

—SIR WINSTON CHURCHILL

Russians will consume marinated mushrooms and vodka, salted herring and vodka, smoked salmon and vodka, salami and vodka, caviar on brown bread and vodka, pickled cucumbers and vodka, cold tongue and vodka, red beet salad and vodka, scallions and vodka—anything and everything and vodka.

—JOURNALIST AND AUTHOR HEDRICK SMITH

If a Russian is in the hills, count your olives.

—GREEK SAYING

Better the devil in your house than a Russian.

—UKRAINIAN SAYING

Do not trust a Hungarian unless he has a third eye in his forehead.
—CZECH SAYING

•

A crab is no fish, and a Greek is no man.
—RUSSIAN SAYING

•

The Greeks—dirty and impoverished descendants of a bunch of
la-de-da fruit salads who invented democracy and then forgot how to
use it while walking around dressed up like girls.
—P. J. O'ROURKE

•

The Japanese have perfected good manners and made them
indistinguishable from rudeness.
—PAUL THEROUX

There are only two kinds of Chinese—those who give bribes, and
those who take them.

—RUSSIAN SAYING

I found the pearl of the Orient slightly less exciting than a rainy
Sunday evening in Rochester.

—S. J. PERELMAN

Harbin is now being called the Chicago of the East.
This is not a compliment to Chicago.

—BRITISH ESSAYIST AND CRITIC MAURICE BARING

Holland is a country where the earth is better than the air; where profit
is sought more than honor; where there is more sense than esprit, more
goodwill than good humor, more prosperity than pleasure, and where a
visit is preferable to a stay for life.

—GERMAN SAYING

Compared with Greece and Italy, Holland is but a platter-faced, cold-gin-and-water country, after all, and a heavy, barge-built, web-footed race are its inhabitants.

—SIR FRANCIS BOND HEAD

The Dutch fall into two quite distinct physical types—the small, corpulent, red-faced Edams and then thinner, paler, larger Goudas.

—ENGLISH HUMORIST AND BROADCASTER ALAN COREN

The indigested vomit of the sea / Fell to the Dutch by just propriety.

—ANDREW MARVELL

God made serpents and rabbits and Armenians.

—TURKISH SAYING

The food in Yugoslavia is fine if you like pork tartare.
—ED BEGLEY JR.

Few things can be less tempting or dangerous than a
Greek woman of the age of thirty.
—IRISH TV WRITER JOHN CARNE

In America, only the successful writer is important, in France all
writers are important, in England no writer is important, and in
Australia you have to explain what a writer is.
—AUTHOR GEOFFREY COTTRELL

Australia may be the only country in the world in which the term
"Academic" is regularly used as a term of abuse.
—DAME LEONIE KRAMER

To live in Australia permanently is rather like going to a party and
dancing all night with your mother.
—TV PERSONALITY BARRY HUMPHRIES

There have been many definitions of hell, but for the English the best
definition is that it is the place where the Germans are the police,
the Swedish are the comedians, the Italians are the defense force,
Frenchmen dig the roads, the Belgians are the pop singers, the Spanish
run the railways, the Turks cook the food, the Irish are the waiters, the
Greeks run the government, and the common language is Dutch.
—SIR DAVID FROST

Chapter
. . . .
VI

Ratting on Writers:
Authors and Their Critics

With the single exception of Homer, there is no eminent writer, not even Sir Walter Scott, whom I can despise so entirely as I despise Shakespeare when I measure my mind against his . . . it would positively be a relief to me to dig him up and throw stones at him.
—GEORGE BERNARD SHAW ON WILLIAM SHAKESPEARE

You ought to be roasted alive, though even
then you would not be to my taste.
—SIR JAMES M. BARRIE TO GEORGE BERNARD SHAW

The way Bernard Shaw believes in himself is very refreshing in these atheistic days when so many people believe in no God at all.
—ISRAEL ZANGWILL ON GEORGE BERNARD SHAW

. . . An unmanly sort of man whose love life seems to have been largely confined to crying in laps and playing mouse.
—W. H. AUDEN ON EDGAR ALLAN POE

The triumph of sugar over diabetes.

—GEORGE JEAN NATHAN ON SIR JAMES M. BARRIE

•

A reptile marking his path wherever he goes and breathing a mildew at everything fresh and fragrant; a midnight ghoul preying on rottenness and repulsive filth. A creature hated by his nearest intimates and bearing his consciousness thereof upon his distorted features and upon his despicable soul.

—WALT WHITMAN ON NEWSPAPER PUBLISHER
JAMES GORDON BENNETT

•

This awful Whitman. This post-mortem poet. This poet with the private soul leaking out of him all the time. All his privacy leaking out in a sort of dribble, oozing into the universe.

—D. H. LAWRENCE ON WALT WHITMAN

What a poor, ignorant, malicious, shortsighted, crapulous mass
is Tom Paine's *Common Sense*.

—JOHN ADAMS

This poem will not reach its destination.

—VOLTAIRE, ON FRENCH POET JEAN-BAPTISTE ROUSSEAU'S
ODE "TO POSTERITY"

We can say of Shakespeare, that never has a man turned so little
knowledge to such great account.

—T. S. ELIOT ON WILLIAM SHAKESPEARE

I haven't any right to criticize books, and I don't do it except when
I hate them. I often want to criticize Jane Austen, but her books
madden me so that I can't conceal my frenzy from the reader; and
therefore I have to stop every time I begin. Every time I read "Pride
and Prejudice," I want to dig her up and hit her over the skull with her
own shin-bone.

—SAMUEL L. CLEMENS

A hack writer who would not have been considered fourth
rate in Europe, who tricked out a few of the old proven sure
fire literary skeletons with sufficient local color to
intrigue the superficial and the lazy.
—WILLIAM FAULKNER ON SAMUEL L. CLEMENS

Miss Austen's novels . . . seem to me vulgar in tone, sterile in
artistic invention, imprisoned in the wretched conventions of English
society, without genius, wit, or knowledge of the world. Never
was life so pinched and narrow.
—RALPH WALDO EMERSON ON JANE AUSTEN

The swish-swash of the press, the bum of impudency, the shambles of
beastliness . . . the toadstool of the realm.
—GABRIEL HARVEY ON THOMAS NASHE, TWO ENGLISH
WRITERS KNOWN FOR THEIR FEUD

The verses, when they were written, resembled nothing so much as spoonfuls of boiling oil, ladled out by a fiendish monkey at an upstairs window upon such of the passers-by whom the wretch had a grudge against.

—WRITER LYTTON STRACHEY ON ALEXANDER POPE

There are two ways of disliking poetry; one way is to dislike it, the other is to read Pope.

—OSCAR WILDE ON ALEXANDER POPE

. . . This enormous dunghill.

—VOLTAIRE ON WILLIAM SHAKESPEARE

. . . A nice, acrid, savage, pathetic old chap.

—I. A. RICHARDS ON ROBERT FROST

. . . A great cow full of ink.

—GUSTAVE FLAUBERT ON GEORGE SAND

The cruelest thing that has happened to Lincoln since he was shot by Booth was to fall into the hands of Carl Sandburg.

—EDMUND WILSON

A poor creature, who has said or done nothing worth a serious man taking the trouble of remembering.

—THOMAS CARLYLE ON PERCY BYSSHE SHELLEY

. . . A lewd vegetarian.

—AUTHOR CHARLES KINGSLEY ON PERCY BYSSHE SHELLEY

Reading Don Quixote can be compared to an indefinite visit from your most impossible senior relative, with all his pranks, dirty habits, unstoppable reminiscences, and terrible cronies. When the experience is over, and the old boy checks out at last. . ., you will shed tears all right; not tears of relief or regret but tears of pride. You made it, despite all that "Don Quixote" could do.
—NOVELIST MARTIN AMIS ON MIGUEL DE CERVANTES

The very pimple of the age's humbug.
—NATHANIEL HAWTHORNE ON WRITER AND POLITICIAN
EDWARD BULWER-LYTTON

To the service of the most wildly eccentric thoughts, he brings the acerbity of a bigot . . . his mental temperament is that of the first Spanish Grand Inquisitor. He is a Torquemada of aesthetics . . . he would burn alive the critic who disagrees with him.
—PHYSICIST, AUTHOR, AND SOCIAL CRITIC
MAX NORDAU ON JOHN RUSKIN

Longfellow is to poetry what the barrel organ is to music.
—AMERICAN LITERARY CRITIC VAN WYCK BROOKS ON HENRY
WADSWORTH LONGFELLOW

He writes his plays for the ages—the ages between five and twelve.
—GEORGE JEAN NATHAN ON GEORGE BERNARD SHAW

. . . A monster, gibbering, shrieking and gnashing
imprecations against mankind.
—WILLIAM MAKEPEACE THACKERAY ON JONATHAN SWIFT

You can gain nothing by reading her. It is like eating snowballs, with
which one can surfeit one's self without satisfying the stomach.
—NAPOLEON BONAPARTE ON MADAME MARIE DE SEVIGNE

Paradise Lost is one of the books which the reader admires
and lays down, and forgets to take up again. Its perusal is
a duty rather than a pleasure.
—**SAMUEL JOHNSON ON JOHN MILTON**

A great author, notwithstanding his Dictionary is imperfect, his
Rambler pompous, his Idler inane, his Lives unjust, his poetry
inconsiderable, his learning common, his ideas vulgar, his Irene a child
of mediocrity, his genius and wit moderate, his precepts worldly, his
politics narrow and his religion bigoted.
—**AMERICAN POLITICIAN ROBERT POTTER ON SAMUEL JOHNSON**

. . . A hyena that wrote poetry on tombs.
—**FRIEDRICH NIETZSCHE ON DANTE ALIGHIERI**

Reading him is like wading through glue.
—**ALFRED, LORD TENNYSON ON BEN JONSON**

Dostoyevsky's lack of taste, his monotonous dealings with persons suffering with pre-Freudian complexes, the way he has of wallowing in the tragic misadventures of human dignity—all this is difficult to admire.

—VLADIMIR NABOKOV

. . . All raw, uncooked, protesting.

—VIRGINIA WOOLF ON ALDOUS HUXLEY

The stupid person's idea of the clever person.

—EZRA BOWEN ON ALDOUS HUXLEY

. . . An idiot child screaming in a hospital.

—H. G. WELLS ON GEORGE BERNARD SHAW

. . . A large shaggy dog just unchained scouring the beaches
of the world and baying at the moon.
—ROBERT LOUIS STEVENSON ON WALT WHITMAN

•

I loathe you. You revolt me stewing in your consumption . . . the
Italians were quite right to have nothing to do with you. You are a
loathsome reptile—I hope you die.
—D. H. LAWRENCE TO SHORT STORY WRITER
KATHERINE MANSFIELD

•

He [looks like] an umbrella left behind at a picnic.
—GEORGE MOORE ON WILLIAM BUTLER YEATS

•

Filth. Nothing but obscenities.
—JOSEPH CONRAD ON D. H. LAWRENCE

What is Conrad but the wreck of Stevenson floating about
in the slipslop of Henry James?
—GEORGE MOORE ON JOSEPH CONRAD

There are a lot of daring people in the world who claimed that Cooper
could write English, but they're all dead now.
—MARK TWAIN ON JAMES FENIMORE COOPER

Here are Johnny Keats' piss-a-bed poetry, and three novels by God
knows whom . . . No more Keats, I entreat: flay him alive; if some of
you don't I must skin him myself: there is no bearing the drivelling
idiotism of the Mankin.
—LORD BYRON

The world is rid of Lord Byron, but the deadly
slime of his touch still remains.
—JOHN CONSTABLE

Wordsworth has left a bad impression wherever he visited in town by his egotism, vanity and bigotry.

—JOHN KEATS ON WILLIAM WORDSWORTH

Mr. Kipling . . . stands for everything in this cankered world which I would wish were otherwise.

—DYLAN THOMAS ON RUDYARD KIPLING

Kipling is a jingo imperialist, he is morally insensitive and aesthetically disgusting.

—WRITER GEORGE ORWELL ON RUDYARD KIPLING

Isn't she a poisonous thing of a woman, lying, concealing, flipping, plagiarising, misquoting and being as clever a crooked literary publicist as ever.

—DYLAN THOMAS ON DAME EDITH SITWELL

I grow bored in France—and the main reason is that everybody here resembles Voltaire . . . the king of nincompoops, the prince of the superficial, the anti-artist, the spokesman of janitresses, the Father Gigone of the editors of *Siècle*.

—CHARLES BAUDELAIRE ON VOLTAIRE

. . . A huge pendulum attached to a small clock.

—RUSSIAN CRITIC IVAN PANIN ON SAMUEL TAYLOR COLERIDGE

I am reading Henry James . . . and feel myself as one entombed in a block of smooth amber.

—VIRGINIA WOOLF

Henry James has a mind—a sensibility—so fine that no mere idea could ever penetrate it.

—T. S. ELIOT

I am reading Proust for the first time. Very poor stuff. I think
he was mentally defective.
—EVELYN WAUGH ON MARCEL PROUST

Lawrence is in a long line of people, beginning with
Heraclitus and ending with Hitler, whose ruling motive
is hatred derived from megalomania, and I am sorry to see
that I was once so far out in estimating him.
—BERTRAND RUSSELL ON D. H. LAWRENCE

Probably Joyce thinks that because he prints all the
dirty little words he is a great hero.
—GEORGE MOORE ON JAMES JOYCE

. . . A louse in the locks of literature.
—ALFRED, LORD TENNYSON ON LITERARY CRITIC
JOHN CHURTON COLLINS

And it is that word "hummy," my darlings, that marks the first place in *The House at Pooh Corner* at which Tonstant Weader fwowed up.
—DOROTHY PARKER ON A. A. MILNE

I invariably miss most of the lines in the last act of an Ibsen play; I always have my fingers in my ears, waiting for the loud report that means that the heroine has just Passed On.
—DOROTHY PARKER ON HENRIK IBSEN

Everything which another man would have hidden, everything the publication of which would have made another man hang himself, was a matter of exaltation to his weak and diseased mind.
—THOMAS BABINGTON MACAULAY ON JAMES BOSWELL

Am reading more of Oscar Wilde. What a tiresome, affected sod.
—NOEL COWARD ON OSCAR WILDE

The affair between Margot Asquith and Margot Asquith will live as
one of the prettiest love stories in all literature.
—DOROTHY PARKER ON MARGOT ASQUITH'S MEMOIRS

What a man Balzac would have been if he had known how to write.
—GUSTAVE FLAUBERT ON HONORÉ DE BALZAC

Nobody can be more clownish, more clumsy and sententiously in bad
taste than Herman Melville.
—D. H. LAWRENCE ON HERMAN MELVILLE

Mr. Lawrence looked like a plaster gnome on a stone toadstool in some
suburban garden . . . he looked as if he had just returned from spending
an uncomfortable night in a very dark cave.
—DAME EDITH SITWELL ON D. H. LAWRENCE

What an old covered wagon she is.
—F. SCOTT FITZGERALD ON GERTRUDE STEIN

•

Gertrude Stein's prose-song is a cold, black suet-pudding.
We can represent it as a cold suet-roll of fabulously reptilian length.
Cut it at any point, it is . . . the same heavy, sticky, opaque mass all
through and all along.
—WRITER WYNDHAM LEWIS ON GERTRUDE STEIN

•

Literary diarrhea.
—NOEL COWARD ON GERTRUDE STEIN

•

It's like reading a bad newspaper or a bad piece in a magazine.
—JOHN IRVING ON TOM WOLFE

It's entertainment, not literature.
—JOHN UPDIKE ON TOM WOLFE

•

There is something silly about a man who wears a white
suit all the time, especially in New York.
—NORMAN MAILER ON TOM WOLFE

•

. . . two old piles of bones.
—TOM WOLFE ON NORMAN MAILER AND JOHN UPDIKE

•

Kerouac lacks discipline, intelligence, honesty and a sense of the
novel. His rhythms are erratic, his sense of character is nil, and he is as
pretentious as a rich whore, sentimental as a lollypop.
—NORMAN MAILER ON JACK KEROUAC

•

That's not writing—that's typing.
—TRUMAN CAPOTE ON JACK KEROUAC

Capote I truly loathed. The way you might loathe an animal. A filthy animal that has found its way into the house.

—GORE VIDAL ON TRUMAN CAPOTE

I seem to be alone in finding him no more than the greatest mind ever to stay in prep school.

—NORMAN MAILER ON J. D. SALINGER

My God, what a clumsy *olla putrida* James Joyce is! Nothing but old fags and cabbage stumps of quotations from the Bible and the rest, stewed in the juice of deliberate, journalistic dirty-mindedness—what old and hard-worked staleness, masquerading as the all-new!

—D. H. LAWRENCE ON JAMES JOYCE

Filth. Nothing but obscenities.

—JOSEPH CONRAD ON D. H. LAWRENCE

I cannot abide Conrad's souvenir shop style and bottled ships and shell necklaces of romanticist clichés.
—VLADIMIR NABOKOV ON JOSEPH CONRAD

•

An enthusiasm for Poe is a mark of a decidedly primitive stage of reflection.
—HENRY JAMES ON EDGAR ALLAN POE

•

Owen's tiny corpus is perhaps the most overrated poetry in the twentieth century.
—POET CRAIG RAINE ON POET WILFRED OWEN

•

He has never been known to use a word that might send a reader to the dictionary.
—WILLIAM FAULKNER ON ERNEST HEMINGWAY

Poor Faulkner. Does he really think big emotions come from big words?
—ERNEST HEMINGWAY ON WILLIAM FAULKNER

He's a full-fledged housewife from Kansas with all the prejudices.
—GORE VIDAL ON TRUMAN CAPOTE

Every word she writes is a lie, including "and" and "the."
—MARY MCCARTHY ON LILLIAN HELLMAN

"The Group" is the best novel the editors of the women's magazines
ever conceived in their secret ambitions.
—NORMAN MAILER ON MARY MCCARTHY

I finished *Ulysses* and think it is a misfire. Genius it has, I think;
but of the inferior water. The book is diffuse. It is brackish. It
is pretentious. It is underbred. [*Ulysses* is] the work of a queasy
undergraduate scratching his pimples.
—VIRGINIA WOOLF ON JAMES JOYCE

To say that Agatha Christie's characters are cardboard cut-outs is an insult to cardboard cut-outs.
—MYSTERY WRITER RUTH RENDELL ON AGATHA CHRISTIE

Is there no beginning to your talents?
—TELEVISION PERSONALITY CLIVE ANDERSON
TO FORMER POLITICIAN AND AUTHOR JEFFREY ARCHER

I cannot take him seriously as a major novelist. I do not think he knows anything about people, nor about himself.
—NORMAN MAILER ON SAUL BELLOW

Saint David Foster Wallace: a generation trying to read him feels smart about themselves, which is part of the whole bullshit package.
—AUTHOR BRET EASTON ELLIS

A terrible writer but he's very successful.

—STEPHEN KING ON JAMES PATTERSON

All American writing gives me the impression that Americans don't care for girls at all. What the American male really wants is two things: he wants to be blown by a stranger while reading a newspaper and he wants to be f****d by his buddy when he's drunk. Everything else is society.

—W. H. AUDEN

Chapter

· · · · · · · · · ·

VII

Mightier than the Sword:
Literary Vitriol

If you will forgive me for being personal—I do not like your face.
—AGATHA CHRISTIE: *MURDER ON THE ORIENT EXPRESS*

•

All morons hate it when you call them a moron.
—J.D. SALINGER: *THE CATCHER IN THE RYE*

•

This wasn't just plain terrible, this was fancy terrible.
This was terrible with raisins in it.
—DOROTHY PARKER: *WOMEN KNOW EVERYTHING!*

•

I desire that we be better strangers.
—WILLIAM SHAKESPEARE: *AS YOU LIKE IT*

Even on Central Avenue, not the quietest dressed street
in the world, he looked about as inconspicuous as a
tarantula on a slice of angel food.
—**RAYMOND CHANDLER**: *FAREWELL MY LOVELY*

Mrs. Joe was a very clean housekeeper, but had an exquisite
art of making her cleanliness more uncomfortable and
unacceptable than dirt itself.
—**CHARLES DICKENS**: *GREAT EXPECTATIONS*

You've got a nice-looking husband.
Maybe I ought to fix you up with him. After all, you're both analysts.
You'd have a lot in common. You could b****r each other under a
picture of Freud.
—**ERICA JONG**: *FEAR OF FLYING*

It's no use telling me that there are bad aunts and good aunts. At the core, they are all alike. Sooner or later, out pops the cloven hoof.

—P. G. WODEHOUSE: *THE CODE OF THE WOOSTERS*

•

"IM GOING TO GET YOU YOU C*** YOU F***ING B*****D. And when I do—The whole world will Know That you destroyed Part of my childhood, TRACEY EMIN"

—TRACEY EMIN: *STRANGELAND*

•

Pack you hence, therefore, you hypocrites, to your sheep-dogs; get you gone, you dissemblers, to the devil! Hay! What, are you there yet? I renounce my part of Papimanie, if I snatch you, Grr, Grrr, Grrrrrr. Avaunt, avaunt! Will you not be gone? May you never shit till you be soundly lashed with stirrup leather, never piss but by the strapado, nor be otherwise warmed than by the bastinado.

—FRANÇOIS RABELAIS: *GARGANTUA AND PANTAGRUEL* (BOOK 3)

First of all, this prince is an idiot, and, secondly, he is a fool—knows
nothing of the world, has no place in it. Whom can he be shown to?
Where can you take him to?
—**FYODOR DOSTOYEVSKY**: *THE IDIOT*

If your brains were dynamite there wouldn't
be enough to blow your hat off.
—**KURT VONNEGUT**: *TIMEQUAKE*

You're a beast and a swine and a bloody, bloody thief!
—**WILLIAM GOLDING**: *LORD OF THE FLIES*

You're not worth the trouble it'd take to hit you. You're not
worth the powder it'd take to blow you up. You're an empty,
hollow f*****g shell of a woman . . .
—**RICHARD YATES**: *REVOLUTIONARY ROAD*

You're history, Donohue. You think countries run the f***ing world!
Go back to f***ing Sunday school.
—JOHN LE CARRE: *THE CONSTANT GARDENER*

•

You blithering idiot! . . . You festering gumboil! You fleabitten fungus! .
. . You bursting blister! You moth-eaten maggot!
—ROALD DAHL: *MATILDA*

•

Just because you have the emotional range of a teaspoon
doesn't mean we all have.
—J. K. ROWLING: *HARRY POTTER AND THE
ORDER OF THE PHOENIX*

Well, well, well, well. If it isn't fat, stinking billygoat Billy-Boy
in poison. How art thou, thy globby bottle of cheap, stinking
chip-oil? Come and get one in the garbles, if you have any
garbles, you eunuch jelly thou.
—ANTHONY BURGESS: *A CLOCKWORK ORANGE*

I misjudged you . . . You're not a moron. You're only
a case of arrested development.
—ERNEST HEMINGWAY: *THE SUN ALSO RISES*

Be silent! Keep your forked tongue behind you teeth. I have not passed
through fire and death to bandy crooked words with a witless worm!
—J. R. R. TOLKIEN: *THE LORD OF THE RINGS*

That is such crap. How dare you be so fraudulently flirtatious, cowardly and dysfunctional? I am not interested in emotional f***wittage. Good-bye.
—**HELEN FIELDING:** *BRIDGET JONES'S DIARY*

•

She looks as if butter wouldn't melt in her mouth.
—**WILLIAM MAKEPEACE THACKERAY:**
THE HISTORY OF PENDENNIS

•

You are the last man in the world I could ever be prevailed upon to marry.
—**JANE AUSTEN:** *PRIDE AND PREJUDICE*

•

The man is as useless as nipples on a breastplate.
—**GEORGE R. R. MARTIN:** *A FEAST FOR CROWS*

Without your art you are nothing. I would have made you famous, splendid, magnificent. The world would have worshipped you, and you would have borne my name. What are you now?

A third-rate actress with a pretty face.

—OSCAR WILDE: *THE PICTURE OF DORIAN GRAY*

•

As for you, little envious prigs, snarling bastards, puny critics, you'll soon have railed your last; go hang yourselves, and choose you out some well-spread oak, under whose shade you may swing in state, to the admiration of the gaping mob; you shall never want rope enough.

—FRANCOIS RABELAIS: *GARGANTUA AND PANTAGRUEL*

•

There's no more faith in thee than in a stewed prune.

—WILLIAM SHAKESPEARE: *HENRY IV*

As it happened, I knew Gartrell. He was a bad painter and a vicious gossip, with a vocabulary composed almost entirely of obscenities, guttural verbs, and the word "postmodernist."

—DONNA TARTT: *THE SECRET HISTORY*

I never saw anybody take so long to dress, and with such little result.

—OSCAR WILDE: *THE IMPORTANCE OF BEING EARNEST*

He's not human; he's an empty space disguised as a human.

—JOHN FOWLES: *THE COLLECTOR*

I did meet David Beckham, though. He held my hand while Posh wasn't looking. She's really rough without makeup.

—KATIE PRICE: *BEING JORDAN*

And she's got brains enough for two, which is the exact quantity the
girl who marries you will need.
—P. G. WODEHOUSE: *THE ADVENTURES OF SALLY*

•

You may be an undigested bit of beef, a blot of mustard, a crumb of
cheese, a fragment of underdone potato. There's more of gravy than of
grave about you, whatever you are!
—CHARLES DICKENS: *A CHRISTMAS CAROL*

•

He gave me a lynched daddy, a crazy mama, a lowdown dog of a step
pa and a sister I probably won't ever see again. Anyhow, I say, the God
I been praying and writing to is a man. And act just like all the other
mens I know. Trifling, forgitful and lowdown.
—ALICE WALKER: *THE COLOR PURPLE*

Martha: Uh . . . you make me puke!
—EDWARD ALBEE: *WHO'S AFRAID OF VIRGINIA WOOLF?*

•

A human being whose life is nurtured in an advantage which has accrued from the disadvantage of other human beings, and who prefers that this should remain as it is, is a human being by definition only, having much more in common with the bedbug, the tapeworm, the cancer, and the scavengers of the deep sea.
—JAMES AGEE: *LET US NOW PRAISE FAMOUS MEN*

•

Come, let us pity those who are better off than we are / Come, my friend, and remember that the rich have butlers and no friends / And we have friends and no butlers.
—EZRA POUND: *THE GARRET*

•

You talk too damn much and too damn much of it is about you.
—RAYMOND CHANDLER: *THE LONG GOODBYE*

Don't fool yourself, my dear. You're much worse than a bitch. You're a saint. Which shows why saints are dangerous and undesirable."
—**AYN RAND**: *THE FOUNTAINHEAD*

The mythology of Einstein shows him as a genius so lacking in magic that one speaks about his thought as of a function analogous to the mechanical making of sausages, the grinding of corn or the crushing of ore.
—**ROLAND BARTHES**: *MYTHOLOGIES*

Don't try to deconstruct it, Carol—it's a phenomenon too abstract for your thought process—it's called humor.
—**WOODY ALLEN**: *CENTRAL PARK WEST*

He is simply a hole in the air.
—**GEORGE ORWELL**: *THE LION AND THE UNICORN:*
SOCIALISM AND THE ENGLISH GENIUS

She's not leaving me! Certainly not for a common swindler who'd have
to steal the ring he put on her finger.
—F. SCOTT FITZGERALD: *THE GREAT GATSBY*

•

As long as she thinks of a man, nobody objects to a woman thinking.
—VIRGINIA WOOLF: *ORLANDO*

•

This liberal doxy must be impaled upon the member
of a particularly large stallion!
—JOHN KENNEDY TOOLE: *A CONFEDERACY OF DUNCES*

•

A deistical prater, fit to sit in the chimney-corner of a pot-house,
and make blasphemous comments on the one greasy newspaper
fingered by beer-swilling tinkers.
—GEORGE ELIOT: *JANET'S REPENTANCE*

If all the girls attending [the Yale prom] were laid end to end,

I wouldn't be at all surprised.

—ALEXANDER WOOLLCOTT: *WHILE ROME BURNS*

●

It's a nasty view of things . . . no wonder you are afraid of yourself and

your own unhappiness.

—D. H. LAWRENCE: *WOMEN IN LOVE*

●

She fitted into my biggest armchair as if it had been built round

her by someone who knew they were wearing armchairs tight

about the hips that season.

—P. G. WODEHOUSE: *MY MAN JEEVES*

●

Choose us. Choose life. Choose mortgage payments; choose washing

machines; choose cars; choose sitting on a couch watching mind-

numbing and spirit-crushing game shows, stuffing f****n' junk food

intae yir mooth. Choose rotting away, pishing and shiteing yersel in a

home, a total f****n' embarrassment tae the selfish, f****d-up brats

ye've produced. Choose life.

—IRVINE WELSH: *TRAINSPOTTING*

My dear, I don't give a damn.
—MARGARET MITCHELL: *GONE WITH THE WIND*

•

Thou art a base, proud, shallow, beggarly, three-suited, hundred-pound,
filthy worsted-stocking knave; a lily-liver'd, action-taking, whoreson,
glass-gazing, superserviceable, finical rogue; one-trunk-inheriting slave;
one that wouldst be a bawd in way of good service, and art nothing but
the composition of a knave, beggar, coward, pandar, and the son and
heir of a mongrel bitch.
—WILLIAM SHAKESPEARE: *KING LEAR*

•

Young man, I am afraid your speech was a trifle short. You could have
said at least one hundred other things, varying the tone of your words.
Let me give you some examples.
In an aggressive tone: "Sir, if I had a nose like that, I would amputate
it!"
Friendly: "When you drink from a cup your nose must get wet. Why
don't you drink from a bowl?"

Descriptive: "Tis a rock! A peak! A cape! No, it's a peninsula!"

Curious: "What is that large container for? To hold your pens and ink?"

Gracious: "How kind you are. You love the little birds so much you
have given them a perch to roost upon."

Truculent: "When you light your pipe and puff smoke from your nose
the neighbors must think the chimney's afire."

Considerate: "Be careful when you bow your head or you might lose
your balance and fall over."

Thoughtful: "Place an umbrella over your nose to keep its color from
fading in the sun."

Arcane: "Sir, only the beast that Aristophanes calls the
hippocampelephantocamelos could have had such a solid lump of flesh
and bone below its forehead."

Cavalier: "A hook to hang your hat upon."

Emphatic: "No breeze, O majestic nose, can give thee cold—save when
the north winds blow."

Dramatic: "When it bleeds, it must be like the Red Sea."

Admiring: "What a fine sign for a perfume shop!"

Lyrical: "Is that a conch shell? And are you Triton risen from the ocean?"

Naïve: "Is that monument open to the public?"

Rustic: "That don't look like a nose. It's either a big cucumber or a little watermelon."

Military: "The enemy is charging! Aim your cannon!"

Practical: "A nose like that has one advantage: it keeps your feet dry in the rain."

•

There, sir, now you have an inkling of what you might have said, had you been a witty man of letters. Unfortunately, you're totally witless and a man of very few letters: only four that spell the word "fool." But even if you had the skill to invent such remarks, you would not have been able to entertain me with them. You would have uttered no more than a quarter of such a jest, the first syllable of the first word, for such jesting is a privilege I only grant myself.

—EDMOND ROSTAND: *CYRANO DE BERGERAC*

Chapter

· · · · · · · · · · ·

VIII

Roil over Beethoven:
Classical Musicians

Far too noisy, my dear Mozart, far too many notes . . .
—ARCHDUKE FERDINAND OF AUSTRIA
ON WOLFGANG AMADEUS MOZART

•

I can compare *Le Carnaval Romain* by Berlioz to nothing
but the caperings and gibberings of a big baboon, over-excited
by a dose of alcoholic stimulus.
—GEORGE TEMPLETON STRONG ON HECTOR BERLIOZ

•

What a good thing this isn't music.
—GIOACHINO ROSSINI ON HECTOR BERLIOZ'S
SYMPHONIE FANTASTIQUE

•

Listening to the fifth symphony of Ralph Vaughan Williams is like
staring at a cow for forty-five minutes.
—AARON COPLAND

A German singer! I should as soon expect to get pleasure

from the neighing of my horse.

—FREDERICK THE GREAT

The first act occupied three hours . . . I enjoyed

that in spite of the singing.

—MARK TWAIN ON RICHARD WAGNER'S *OPERA PARSIFAL*

Rossini would have been a great composer if his teacher

had spanked him enough on the backside.

—LUDWIG VAN BEETHOVEN ON GIOACHINO ROSSINI

I liked your opera. I think I will set it to music.

—LUDWIG VAN BEETHOVEN TO AN UNNAMED COMPOSER

After Rossini dies, who will there be to promote his music?
—RICHARD WAGNER ON GIOACHINO ROSSINI

Beethoven always sounds like the upsetting of bags—with
here and there a dropped hammer.
—JOHN RUSKIN ON LUDWIG VAN BEETHOVEN

Rachmaninov's immortalising totality was his scowl.
He was a six-and-a-half-foot scowl.
—IGOR STRAVINSKY ON SERGEY RACHMANINOFF

All you need to write like him is a large bottle of ink.
—IGOR STRAVINSKY ON OLIVIER MESSIAEN

It is the most insipid and base parody on music.
—PYOTR TCHAIKOVSKY ON MODEST MUSSORGSKY'S
BORIS GODUNOV

It's beautiful and boring. Too many pieces finish too long after the end.
—IGOR STRAVINSKY ON
GEORGE FRIDERIC HANDEL'S *THEODORA*

. . . The musical equivalent of St Pancras Station.
—SIR THOMAS BEECHAM ON EDWARD ELGAR

It's bad when they don't perform your operas—but
when they do, it's far worse.
—CHARLES-CAMILLE SAINT-SAËNS TO DAME EDITH SMYTHE

. . . A tub of pork and beer.

—HECTOR BERLIOZ ON GEORGE FRIDERIC HANDEL

●

His wantonness is not vicious. It is that of a great baby, rather tirelessly addicted to dressing himself up as Handel or Beethoven and making a prolonged and intolerable noise.

—GEORGE BERNARD SHAW ON JOHANNES BRAHMS

●

Art is long and life is short; here is evidently the explanation of a Brahms symphony.

—EDWARD LOME ON JOHANNES BRAHMS

●

Berlioz, musically speaking, is a lunatic; a classical composer only in Paris, the great city of quacks. His music is simply and disguisedly nonsense.

—DRAMATIC AND MUSICAL REVIEW ON HECTOR BERLIOZ

The audience expected the ocean. Something big, something colossal,
but they were served instead with some agitated water in a saucer.
—MUSIC CRITIC LOUIS SCHNEIDER
ON MAURICE RAVEL'S *LA MER*

•

He likes what is coarse, unpolished, and ugly.
—PYOTR TCHAIKOVSKY ON MODEST MUSSORGSKY

•

. . . A composer for one right hand.
—RICHARD WAGNER ON FRÉDÉRIC CHOPIN

•

He gives me the impression of being a spoilt child.
—CLARA SCHUMANN ON FRANZ LISZT

I like Wagner's music better than any other music; it is so loud that one
can talk the whole time without people hearing what one says.
—OSCAR WILDE

All Bach's last movements are like the running of a sewing machine.
—SIR ARNOLD BAX ON JOHANN SEBASTIAN BACH

Anton Bruckner wrote the same symphony nine times [ten actually],
trying to get it right. He failed.
—EDWARD ABBEY

It's like a lot of yaks jumping around!
—SIR THOMAS BEECHAM ON BEETHOVEN'S *SYMPHONY NO. 7*

Wagner's music is better than it sounds.
—MARK TWAIN ON RICHARD WAGNER

Is Wagner actually a man? Is he not rather a disease? Everything he
touches falls ill: He has made music sick.

—FRIEDRICH WILHELM NIETZSCHE ON RICHARD WAGNER

I love Wagner, but the music I prefer is that of a cat hung
up by its tail outside a window and trying to stick to the
panes of glass with its claws.

—CHARLES BAUDELAIRE ON RICHARD WAGNER

Of all the bete, clumsy, blundering, boggling, baboon-blooded stuff
that I ever saw on a human stage, that last night beat—as far as the
story and acting went—all the affected, sapless, soulless, beginningless,
endless, topless, bottomless, topsiturviest, tuneless, scrabble-pipiest-
tongs and boniest-doggerel of sounds I ever endured the deadliness of,
that eternity of nothing was deadliest, as far as its sound went.

—JOHN RUSKIN ON RICHARD WAGNER

What a giftless bastard!
—PYOTR TCHAIKOVSKY ON JOHANNES BRAHMS

•

Handel is only fourth rate. He is not even interesting.
—PYOTR TCHAIKOVSKY ON GEORGE FRIDERIC HANDEL

•

If he'd been making shell cases during the war, it
would have been better for music.
—CHARLES-CAMILLE SAINT-SAËNS ON MAURICE RAVEL

•

I liked the opera very much. Everything but the music.
—BENJAMIN BRITTEN ON IGOR STRAVINSKY'S
THE RAKE'S PROGRESS

•

He'd be better off shoveling snow than scribbling on manuscript paper.
—RICHARD STRAUSS ON ARNOLD SCHOENBERG

. . . Bach on the wrong notes.

—COMPOSER SERGE PROKOFIEV ON IGOR STRAVINSKY

•

God tells me how the music should sound, but you stand in the way.

—ARTURO TOSCANINI, TO AN ORCHESTRA MUSICIAN

•

He tried Debussy's *La Mer* once. It came out as Das Merde.

—ORCHESTRA MEMBER ON CONDUCTOR GEORGE SZELL

•

Madam, you have between your legs an instrument capable of giving

pleasure to thousands and all you can do is scratch it.

—SIR THOMAS BEECHAM, TO A CELLIST

Why do you always insist on playing when I'm trying to conduct?
—EUGENE ORMANDY

A tenor is not a man, but a disease.
—CONDUCTOR HANS VON BÜLOW

. . . A glorified bandmaster.

—SIR THOMAS BEECHAM ON ARTURO TOSCANINI

English sopranos sound as if they subsisted on seaweed. English tenors
sound like yawning giraffes.
—SIR THOMAS BEECHAM

Her singing reminds me of a cart coming downhill with the brake on.
—SIR THOMAS BEECHAM ON A SOPRANO

Chapter

. . . .

IX

Pop Poop: Pop Musicians

Coldplay are the dictionary definition of corporate rock. The singer is about as weird as Phil Collins. They are career rock personified. EMI should've signed Otis the Aadvark instead.

—MUSIC INDUSTRY EXECUTIVE ALAN MCGEE

•

Paul Simon's lyrics alternate between nauseating poeticism . . . and trashy folksiness and are set to his and Garfunkel's music that is not so much rock as rock bottom. [*The Graduate* director Mike] Nichols keeps reprising these decompositions until the soundtrack resembles the streets of New York during the garbage collectors' strike.

—FILM CRITIC JOHN SIMON

•

Taking your clothes off, doing sexy dancing and marrying a rich footballer must be very gratifying. Your mother must be so proud. Stupid bitch.

—LILY ALLEN ON PERFORMER CHERYL COLE

. . . Bambi with testosterone.

—MUSIC CRITIC OWEN GLEIBERMAN ON PRINCE

•

Bob [Dylan] is not authentic at all. He's a plagiarist,

and his name and voice are fake.

—JONI MITCHELL

•

Play us a medley of your hit.

—OSCAR LEVANT TO GEORGE GERSHWIN

•

. . . mostly just sounds constipated.

—*PITCHFORK* ON BECK

•

I don't mean this in a bad way, but he was very much a chauvinist pig.

—DOLLY PARTON ON SINGER PORTER WAGONER

If Morrissey says not to eat meat, then I'll eat meat — that's
how much I hate Morrissey.
—RIVAL POP MUSICIAN ROBERT SMITH

. . . trying to steal money from young alternative kids' pockets.
—*NME* ON PEARL JAM

I can't wait for [Britney Spears'] career to be over so
she can serve me coffee at a 7-Eleven.
—JOAN RIVERS

Music journalists like Elvis Costello because music journalists look like
Elvis Costello.
—DAVID LEE ROTH

I get really tired of their pompousness [sic] . . . We've played some shows with them and they really treat people like shit. People treat Arcade Fire like they're the greatest thing ever and they get away with it . . . They have good tunes, but they're p***ks, so f**k 'em.

—ROCK MUSICIAN WAYNE COYNE

•

I'm not quite sure who this person is, to be honest. I don't know if it is a man or a woman.

—CHRISTINA AGUILERA ON LADY GAGA

•

Back in the UK things weren't going quite so well for Eoghan Quigg, who . . . two weeks ago released the worst album in the history of recorded sound. . . . his self-titled album would be fairly bad, but it's not just bad in the way this sort of album is usually bad. It's an objectively bad album so bad that it would count as a new low for popular culture were it possible to class as either culture . . . or popular . . .

—JOURNALIST PETER ROBINSON

A malicious guy . . . will step on anybody's face to succeed, and cross any line of decency.

—COMPOSER AND ARRANGER TRENT REZNOR ON MARILYN MANSON

She looks like a f***ing fairground stripper.

—PERFORMER ELTON JOHN ON MADONNA

There was this other group warming up . . . and they were terrible. I said, 'Shut them c***s up!' And they were still warming up, so I threw a bottle at them . . . I just thought they were a load of retarded Irish folk singers.

—SINGER AND SONGWRITER MARK E. SMITH ON MUMFORD & SONS

Mick Jagger could French-kiss a moose. He has child-bearing lips.

—JOAN RIVERS

Where's the baby? In the closet with an IV?
—MUSICIAN AND WRITER KATHLEEN HANNA
ON COURTNEY LOVE

•

They even have discordant jams with bass and guitar reeling like
velocitized speedfreaks all over each other's musical perimeters yet
never quite finding synch—just like Cream! But worse.
—MUSIC CRITIC LESTER BANGS ON BLACK SABBATH

•

He was so mean it hurt him to go to the bathroom.
—MOVIE ACTRESS BRITT EKLAND ON ROD STEWART

•

. . . the worst song I've ever heard.
—ZAC BROWN ON LUKE BRYAN'S "THAT'S MY KIND OF NIGHT"

He said he wanted to bring ballet to the working classes. What a c***.

—ROCK MUSICIAN PAUL WELLER ON FREDDIE MERCURY

Boy George is all England needs—another queen who can't dress.

—JOAN RIVERS

They're really talentless people, and they write crap music . . .

—KURT COBAIN ON GUNS N' ROSES

I'm forever near a stereo saying, "What the f*** is this garbage?" And
the answer is always the Red Hot Chili Peppers.

—NICK CAVE

. . . an uninteresting writer, vocalist, and bass player [with songs that
were] boring melodically, harmonically, and lyrically.
—ROLLING STONE ON PINK FLOYD'S ROGER WATERS

•

Morrissey writes wonderful song titles, but sadly
he often forgets to write the song.
—ELVIS COSTELLO

•

This dude is the herpes of music. Once you
think it's gone, it comes back.
—ROCK SINGER BILLY JOE ARMSTRONG ON PSY

•

He looks like Zorro on doughnuts.
—NOEL GALLAGHER ON JACK WHITE

A little short ego-ed f****r who I had a feeling didn't like people of his own race and wanted to be white and taller.
—RICK JAMES ON PRINCE

•

When he did Live Aid, which made them a worldwide group . . . he looked out and [saw] that black girl in the middle of all them people, and she's from Hackney or something, and he was like, "Here's a great shot for me around the world to show I'm Mr. Africa." It's like colonialist times with a big white hat.
—ROCK SINGER IAN BROWN ON BONO

•

The [hard rock] genre has unquestionably hit its all-time low.
—MUSIC JOURNALIST BILLY ALTMAN ON AC/DC

•

Bob Geldof is a nauseating character. Band Aid was the most self-righteous platform ever in the history of popular music.
—MORRISSEY

A vile, hideous human being with no redeeming qualities.
—**BOY GEORGE ON MADONNA**

All that money, and he's still got hair like a f*****g dinner lady.
—**BOY GEORGE ON ELTON JOHN**

Nobody wants to listen to their grandpa's music. And I don't care how many of these old farts around Nashville are going, "My God, that ain't country!" Well that's because you don't buy records anymore, jackass. The kids do, and they don't want to buy the music you were buying.
—**BLAKE SHELTON ON THE OLDER GENERATION OF COUNTRY SINGERS**

Marie Osmond is so pure, not even Moses could even part her knees.
—**JOAN RIVERS**

What has he ever done except throw his baby off a f****n' ledge and
write a song about it?
—ROCK MUSICIAN ANTON NEWCOMBE ON ERIC CLAPTON

This English quintet's debut doesn't really deliver anything you haven't
heard before, steering too close to Smiths-like melodies and trying ever
so hard to be depressed in the way the Cure popularized.
—THE *LOS ANGELES TIMES* ON RADIOHEAD

It's like a monkey with arthritis trying to go on stage and look young.
—ELTON JOHN ON KEITH RICHARDS

His writing is limited to songs for dead blondes.
—KEITH RICHARDS ON ELTON JOHN [THE REFERENCE
IS TO THE LATE PRINCESS DIANA.]

He's just sub-mediocre kind of [guy] who does this "nice guy" nonsense.
—COURTNEY LOVE ON DAVE GROHL

•

She's an ugly f*****g bitch.
—DAVE GROHL ON COURTNEY LOVE

In a nutshell, personally I consider him a cancer and better removed, avoided, and the less anyone heard of him or his supporters, the better.
—AXL ROSE ON SLASH

•

An excess of praise has been heaped upon the band by tastemakers looking to chew up and spit out the next underground icon.
—*DUSTED* MAGAZINE ON ARCADE FIRE

I'm sick and tired of these bands like Carlos Santana looking at his shoes and thinking that's a rock concert.
—GENE SIMMONS ON SANTANA

•

No one even thinks about the Doors any more—such is fame.
—ROBERT CHRISTGAU

Chapter

· · · · · · · · · · ·

X

Bass and Vile:
Musicians and Their Instruments

Q: How do you make musicians complain?

A: Pay them.

Q: How many conductors does it take to screw in a light bulb?

A: No one knows—no one ever looks at him.

Q: What's the difference between a pianist and God?

A: God doesn't think he's a pianist.

Q: How many drummers does it take to change a light bulb?

A: "Oops, I broke it!"

Q: What's the difference between terrorists and accordion players?

A: Terrorists have sympathizers.

Q: How many folk singers does it take to change a light bulb?

A: Six—one to change it and five to sing about how good the old one was.

Q: What do you call a beautiful woman on a trombonist's arm?

A: A tattoo.

Q: What's the difference between a banjo and an onion?

A: Nobody cries when you chop up a banjo.

Q: What do you call a drummer in a three-piece suit?

A: The defendant.

Q: What do clarinetists use for birth control?

A: Their personalities.

Q: What did the drummer get on his IQ test?

A: Saliva.

Q: What do you call a guitar player without a girlfriend?

A: Homeless.

Q: What's the similarity between a drummer and a philosopher?

A: They both perceive time as an abstract concept.

•

Q: What is the difference between a drummer and a vacuum cleaner?

A: You have to plug one of them in before it sucks.

•

Q: Why do some people have an instant aversion to banjo players?

A: It saves time in the long run.

•

Q: What's the difference between a folk guitar player and a large pizza?

A: A large pizza can feed a family of four.

•

Q: What's the difference between a jet airplane and a trumpet?

A: About three decibels.

•

Q: What's the latest crime wave in New York City?

A: Drive-by trombone solos.

Q: What's the definition of a minor second interval?

A: Two soprano sax players reading off the same part.

Q: What is another term for trombone?

A: A wind-driven, manually operated, pitch approximator.

Q: How do you get an oboist to play A flat?

A: Take the batteries out of his electronic tuner.

Q: What is the dynamic range of a bass trombone?

A: On or off.

Q: What's the difference between a SCUD missile and a bad oboist?

A: A bad oboist can kill you.

Q: Why do clarinetists leave their cases on the dashboard?

A: So they can park in the handicapped zones.

Q: What's the definition of perfect pitch?

A: When you toss a banjo in the garbage and it hits an accordion.

Q: What's the difference between an opera singer and a pit bull?

A: Lipstick.

Q: Why do people play trombone?

A: Because they can't move their fingers and read music at the same time.

Q: How does a violist's brain cell die?

A: Alone.

Q: What do you call a guitar player that only knows two chords?

A: A music critic.

Q: How do you keep your violin from being stolen?

A: Put it in a viola case.

Q: What's the difference between a saxophone and a chainsaw?

A: You can tune a chainsaw.

Q: What will you never say about a banjo player?

A: "That's the banjo player's Porsche."

Q: What do a viola and a lawsuit have in common?

A: Everyone is relieved when the case is closed.

Q: Why are harps like elderly parents?

A: Both are unforgiving and hard to get into and out of cars.

Q: How many trumpet players does it take to pave a driveway?

A: Seven . . . if you lay them out correctly.

Q: What's the difference between an oboe and a bassoon?

A: You can hit a baseball farther with a bassoon.

Q: How are a banjo player and a blind javelin thrower alike?

A: Both command immediate attention and alarm,

and force everyone to move out of range.

Q: What's the best recording of the *Walton Viola Concerto*?

A: "Music Minus One"

Q: What's the difference between a Wagnerian

soprano and a baby elephant?

A: Eleven pounds.

Q: Why are a violist's fingers like lightning?

A: They rarely strike the same spot twice.

Q: How many steel guitar players does it take to screw in a light bulb?

A: Thirteen—one to do it, and twelve to stand around and say,

"Phhhwt! I can do that!"

Tuba player: "Did you hear my last recital?"

Music critic: "I hope so."

◉

Q: What's the difference between alto clef and Greek?

A: Some conductors actually read Greek.

◉

Q: How many concertmasters does it take to change a light bulb?

A: Just one, but it takes four movements.

◉

Q: What do you call a tuba player who correctly notices the
key signature?

A: Astute.

◉

Q: What do you call a tuba player playing in the correct key signature?

A: Gifted.

◉

Q: How can a drummer and a conductor avoid rhythm conflicts?

A: Work separate concert halls.

Q: How does a young man become a member of a high school chorus?
A: On the first day of school he goes into the wrong classroom.

Q: What do you call a hundred conductors at the bottom of the ocean?
A: A good start.

Q: Three conductors went down in a plane crash. Who survived?
A: Mozart.

Q: What's the difference between a lawnmower and a viola?
A: Vibrato.

Q: How can you tell when a singer is at your door?
A: They can't find the key, and they never know when to come in.

Q: How do you get two bass players to play in unison?
A: Hand them charts a half-step apart.

Q: What's the difference between a dead chicken in the road, and a
dead trombonist in the road?

A: There's a remote chance the chicken was on its way to a gig.

Q: What do you call someone who hangs around with musicians?

A: A vocalist.

Q: If you see a conductor and a violist in the middle of the road, who
would you run over first?

A: The conductor—business before pleasure.

Q: How do you get a guitarist to play softer?

A: Place a sheet of music in front of him.

Q: Why can't voice majors have colostomies?

A: Because they can't find shoes to match the bag.

Q: What do you do if you see a bleeding drummer running around in your back yard?

A: Stop laughing and shoot again.

•

Q: What's the perfect weight of a conductor?

A: Three-and-a-half pounds, including the urn.

•

Q: What do all great conductors have in common?

A: They're all dead.

•

Q: What's the definition of optimism?

A: A bass trombonist with a beeper.

•

Q: What do you do if you run over a bass player?

A: Back up.

•

Q: How do you reduce wind-drag on a trombonist's car?

A: Take the Domino's Pizza sign off the roof

Q: How do you get a clarinetist out of a tree?

A: Cut the noose.

Q: What do you throw a drowning electric bass player?

A: His amp.

Q: How do you get a three-piece horn section to play in tune?

A: Shoot two of them.

Q: What's the difference between a bull and a band?

A: The bull has the horns in the front and the asshole in the back.

Q: How many vocalists does it take to screw in a bulb?

A: None. They hold the bulb over their head and the world revolves around them.

Q: How many drummers does it take to screw in a bulb?

A: None. They have machines for that now.

Q: How can you tell if the stage is level?

A: The drool comes out of both sides of the drummer's mouth.

Q: How do you get a trombonist off of your porch?

A: Pay him for the pizza.

Q: What's the last thing a drummer says before
he gets kicked out of a band?

A: "When do we get to play *my* songs?"

Q: What do you call a musician with a college degree?

A: Night manager at McDonald's.

Q: Why are violas larger than violins?

A: They aren't. Violists' heads are smaller.

Q: How are trumpet players like pirates?

A: They're both murder on the high Cs.

Q: A violin and a viola are both in a burning building in the same room. Which burns first?

A: The violin, because the viola was in its case.

Q: What's the difference between a dog and a violinist?

A: A dog knows when to quit scratching.

Q: How do you get a trumpet to sound like a French horn?

A: Put your hand in the bell and play a lot of wrong notes.

Q: How does one trumpet player greet another?

A: "Hi. I'm better than you."

Q: How do you know when a drummer is at your door?

A: He speeds up when he's knocking.

Q: How many guitar players does it to take to change a lightbulb?

A: Five—One to change it and four to say they

could have done it better.

•

Young child to mother: "Mom, when I grow up I'd

like to be a musician."

Mother: "You can't do both."

•

Two brass players walked out of a bar . . .

Chapter

· · · · · · · · · · ·

XI

Smear Campaign: Artists' Insults

There is one thing on earth more terrible than English music and that is English painting.

—GERMAN POET AND CRITIC HEINRICH HEINE

•

They are so damn "intellectual" and rotten that I can't stand them anymore . . . I'd rather sit on the floor in the market of Toluca and sell tortillas, than have anything to do with those "artistic" bitches of Paris.

—FRIDA KAHLO ON THE SURREALISTS

•

Matisse! What is a Matisse? A balcony with a big red flowerpot falling all over it.

—PABLO PICASSO ON HENRI MATISSE

•

His *Pygmalion and Galatea in the Lowther Arcadia (No. 49)* has all that wax-doll grace of treatment that is so characteristic of his best work, and is eminently suggestive of the President's earnest and continual struggles to discover the difference between chalk and colour.

—OSCAR WILDE ON PAINTER AND
SEULPTOR SIR FREDERIC LEIGHTON

It resembles a tortoiseshell cat having a fit in a plate of tomatoes.

—MARK TWAIN ON J. M. W. TURNER'S *THE SLAVE SHIP*

Oh, I think he's great. He makes such great lunches.

—ANDY WARHOL ON PAINTER JASPER JOHNS

Completely idiotic critics have for several years used the name of Piet Mondrian as though he represented the sum mum of all spiritual activity. They quote him in every connection. Piet for architecture, Piet for poetry, Piet for mysticism, Piet for philosophy, Piet's whites, Piet's yellows, Piet, Piet, Piet . . . Well I, Salvador, will tell you this, that Piet with one "i" less would have been nothing but pet, which is the French word for fart.

—SALVADOR DALÍ

"What a genius, that Picasso . . . It's a pity he doesn't paint."

—MARC CHAGALL ON PABLO PICASSO

To my eye Rubens's coloring is most contemptible. His shadows are of a filthy brown somewhat the color of excrement.

—WILLIAM BLAKE ON PETER PAUL RUBENS

•

My God, they've shot the wrong person.

—SCULPTOR JAMES PRYDE REACTING TO SIR GEORGE FRAMPTON'S STATUE OF NURSE EDITH CAVELL, WHO WAS ASSASSINATED DURING WORLD WAR I

•

He bores me. He ought to have stuck to his flying machines.

—PIERRE-AUGUSTE RENOIR ON LEONARDO DA VINCI

•

. . . a life passed among pictures makes not a painter—else the policeman in the National Gallery might assert himself. As well allege that he who lives in a library must needs die a poet. Let not Mr. Ruskin flatter himself that more education makes the difference between himself and the policeman when both stand gazing in the Gallery.

—JAMES MCNEILL WHISTLER ON JOHN RUSKIN

. . . A decorator tainted with insanity.

—PAINTER AND TEACHER KENYON COX ON PAUL GAUGUIN

•

As for M. Cezanne, his name will be forever linked with the most memorable artistic joke of the last fifteen years.

—POET AND ART CRITIC CAMILLE MAUCLAIR ON PAUL CÉZANNE

•

He will never be anything but a dauber.

—RENAISSANCE ARTIST TITIAN COMMENTING ON RIVAL ARTIST, TINTORETTO

•

His pictures seem to resemble not pictures but a sample book of patterns of linoleum.

—BRITISH JURIST CYRIL ASQUITH ON PAUL KLEE

I have been to it and am pleased to find it

more odious than I ever dared hope.

—SAMUEL BUTLER ON A DANTE GABRIEL ROSSETTI EXHIBITION

I have seen and heard much of Cockney impudence before now; but

never expected to hear a coxcomb ask two hundred guineas for flinging

a pot of paint in the public's face.

—JOHN RUSKIN ON JAMES MCNEILL WHISTLER

I mock thee not, though I by thee am mocked; Thou call'st me

madman, but I call thee blockhead.

—WILLIAM BLAKE ON SCULPTOR JOHN FLAXMAN

You're a killer of art, you're a killer of beauty, you're even a killer of

laughter. I can't bear your work!

—ARTIST WILLEM DE KOONING TO ANDY WARHOL

If people dug up remains of this civilisation a thousand years hence, and found Epstein's statues . . . they would think we were just savages.
—NOVELIST DORIS LESSING ON SCULPTOR JACOB EPSTEIN

I've never liked his things very much, except the very, very early things . . . I loathe them. I can never see what there is to it, with all those squalid little forms. I can't bear the drawings either—I absolutely hate his line. I find his line sickly.
—FRANCIS BACON ON HENRI MATISSE

If this is art, it must be ostracized as the poets were banished from Plato's republic.
—BRITISH MILITARY OFFICER ROBERT ROSS ON VINCENT VAN GOGH

It makes me look as if I were straining a stool.
—SIR WINSTON CHURCHILL ON GRAHAM SUTHERLAND'S PORTRAIT

Just explain to Monsieur Renoir that the torso of a woman is not a mass of decomposing flesh, its green and violet spots indicating the state of complete putrefaction of a corpse.
—SCULPTOR ALBERT WOLFF ON PIERRE-AUGUSTE RENOIR

I wouldn't have noticed it except that it was so big.
—EDGAR DEGAS ON GEORGES-PIERRE SEURAT

He finished modern art at one blow by outuglying, alone, in a single day, the ugly that all others combined turned out in several years.
—SALVADOR DALÍ ON PABLO PICASSO

Jackson Pollock's paintings might be very pretty but they're just decoration. I always think they look like old lace.
—PAINTER FRANCIS BACON

Picasso is altogether bad, completely beside the point from the beginning except for Cubist period and even that half misunderstood. . . . Ugly. Old-fashioned vulgar without sensitivity, horrible in color or non-color. Very bad painter once and for all.

—SCULPTOR ALBERTO GIACOMETTI ON PABLO PICASSO

The indigestion that goes with fish soup . . .

—SALVADOR DALÍ ON JACKSON POLLOCK'S PAINTING STYLE

I began a happening in New York by announcing in front of three-thousand spectators that Cézanne was a catastrophe of awkwardness—a painter of decrepit structures of the past. I was applauded, principally because nobody knew who Cézanne was.

—SALVADOR DALÍ

Caravaggio's art is painting for lackeys. This man has come into the world to destroy painting.

—ARTIST NICOLAS POUSSIN ON CARAVAGGIO

Everything he knew, he learned from me.

—MICHELANGELO ON RIVAL ARTIST RAPHAEL

I never in my life saw more horrible things. They do not observe drawing nor form but give you an impression of what they call nature. It was worse than the Chamber of Horrors.

—ART CRITIC J. ALDEN WEIR ON
THE FRENCH IMPRESSIONISTS

Rossetti is not a painter. Rossetti is a ladies maid.

—JAMES MCNEILL WHISTLER ON DANTE GABRIEL ROSSETTI

The properties of his figures are sometimes such as might be corrected by a common sign painter.

—ARTIST WILLIAM HOGARTH ON ANTONIO DA CORREGGIO

This is not amusing, it is dismaying and disheartening. The other day, someone attributed to me the statement that "the human race was nearing insanity." I never said that, but if anyone is trying to convince me that this is "modern art," and that it is representative of our time, I would be obliged to think that statement is true.

—ARTIST KENYON COX ON HENRI MATISSE'S PAINTING *THE RED STUDIO*

It's flat, it isn't modeled. It's like the Queen of Hearts after a bath.

—GUSTAVE COURBET ON EDOUARD MANET'S *OLYMPIA*

My dear Whistler, you leave your pictures in such a sketchy, unfinished state. Why don't you ever finish them?

—FREDERIC LEIGHTON ON JAMES MCNEILL WHISTLER

My dear Leighton, why do you ever begin yours?

—JAMES MCNEILL WHISTLER ON FREDERIC LEIGHTON

Chapter

. . . .

XII

Bad Actors:
Theater and Movie Reviews

The jokes were so old the writers must have swept them out of an attic,

and the cast was found by stopping every third person on the street.

—BROOKS ATKINSON ON *HELLZAPOPPIN'*

Amateur Night at Camp Karefree.

—THE *NEW YORK POST* REVIEW OF *WISH YOU WERE HERE*

Kismet has not been written. It has been assembled from a storehouse

of spare parts.

—BROOKS ATKINSON

Voyeurs of the city unite, you have nothing to lose but your brains.

—THEATER CRITIC CLIVE BARNES ON *OH! CALCUTTA*

Apparently the understudy had to go because of her throat;

I suppose someone threatened to cut it.

—MRS. PATRICK CAMPBELL ON AN UNKNOWN ACTRESS

If Benji were in this production, he wouldn't give a convincing performance as a dog.

—FORMER CRITIC TOM BOEKER ON *MEDEA*, BLACK ENSEMBLE

Tallulah Bankhead barged down the Nile last night as Cleopatra and sank.

—THEATER CRITIC JOHN MASON BROWN

Massey won't be satisfied until he's assassinated.

—GEORGE S. KAUFMAN SUGGESTING THAT RAYMOND MASSEY WAS OVERPLAYING THE TITLE ROLE IN *ABE LINCOLN IN ILLINOIS*

I always said that I'd like Barrymore's acting till the cows came home. Well, ladies and gentleman, last night the cows came home.

—GEORGE JEAN NATHAN ON JOHN BARRYMORE

The *House Beautiful* is, for me, the play lousy.
—DOROTHY PARKER

•

. . . A great actress, from the waist down.
—ACTRESS DAME MADGE KENDAL COMMENTING ON RIVAL
ACTRESS SARAH BERNHARDT

•

Me no Leica.
—WALTER KERR ON *I AM A CAMERA*

•

I thought the play was frightful, but I saw it under particularly
unfortunate circumstances. The curtain was up.
—GEORGE S. KAUFMAN

In a desperate attempt to report some favorable news about this production, I'm afraid all I can say is that the show is over in less than an hour. Also, there's a fine Chinese restaurant a couple blocks north of the theater. I recommend the orange beef, with shrimp toast as an appetizer. Bring your own wine or beer. The service, however, is slow, hopefully slow enough that you'll miss the show altogether.

—TOM BOEKER ON *FOUR PORTRAITS OF MOTHERS*

Movies:

Retaining the British accent that makes her even more of an outsider in this scary New World, [Emily] Blunt convinces completely as a drunken fish out of water.

—MARK KERMODE ON *THE GIRL ON THE TRAIN*

Absolute cack: appallingly written, witlessly directed and sung as if by mice being tortured. It makes Teletubbies look like *The Iliad* in comparison.

—MOVIE CRITIC STEPHEN POLLARD ON *MAMMA MIA!*

I would rather turn my head and cough than see any
part of *Patch Adams* again.
—GENE SISKEL

•

I had a colonoscopy once, and they let me watch it on TV. It was more
entertaining than *The Brown Bunny*.
—ROGER EBERT

•

Susannah York is unconvincing at everything:
lesbianism, childishness, acting . . .
—JOHN SIMON ON *THE KILLING OF SISTER GEORGE*

•

I entered the theatre in the bloom of youth and emerged with a family
of field mice living in my long, white moustache. (The film) is an
entirely inappropriate length for what is essentially a home video of
gay men playing with giant Barbie dolls.
—MOVIE CRITIC LINDY WEST ON *SEX AND THE CITY 2*

It is a film so awe-inspiringly wooden that it is basically a fire risk.
—MOVIE CRITIC PETER BRADSHAW ON *GRACE OF MONACO*

He decided to make it exactly as it stood; he crammed [Henry] James's
words into Cybill's [Shepherd] mouth like fish into a letterbox.
—FREDERIC RAPHAEL ON *DAISY MILLER*

Freddy Got Fingered didn't merely scrape the bottom of the barrel, it
doesn't deserve to be mentioned in the same sentence as barrels.
—ROGER EBERT

If I had to catalog all the moronic plot turns in *The Day After
Tomorrow*, we'd be here until the next ice age.
—MOVIE CRITIC DAVID EDELSTEIN

If there are ten films worse than *Bride Wars* this year, I quit . . .
Everyone will tell you it's a chick flick. Only in the sense that if you
ground it up and fed it to battery hens it might be better served than
running it through a projector.
—MARK KERMODE

What can you say about a sequel that
Steve Guttenberg won't even appear in?
—LEONARD MALTIN ON *POLICE ACADEMY 5*

Built to make money but hardly worthy of serious examination. *Avatar*
isn't only critic-proof, it resists serious criticism. You might as well
analyze a beach ball.
—MOVIE CRITIC PHILIP MARTIN

Even more unpleasant, though, is Mimsy Farmer's breathy Marilyn Monroe-Jackie Kennedy English, in which "charcoal," for instance, is pronounced "chuhkuh," the uhs representing gusts of breath. An altogether dispensable girl, this Mimsy, looking and acting like a cross between Sandy Dennis and a young Lizabeth Scott, with added suggestions of Jean Seberg and a death's-head.

—JOHN SIMON ON *MORE*

Fred Astaire looks as if he has just rolled out of his tomb, and Gene Kelly sports a toupee that looks borrowed from Howard Cosell for the occasion.

—MOVIE CRITIC MATT BAILEY ON *THAT'S ENTERTAINMENT PART 2*

(*Revenge of the Sith*) marks a distinct improvement on the last two episodes, *The Phantom Menace* and *Attack of the Clones* . . . but only in the same way that dying from natural causes is preferable to crucifixion.

—MOVIE CRITIC ANTHONY LANE

Speaking in my official capacity as a Pulitzer Prize winner, Mr. Schneider, your movie sucks.

—ROGER EBERT ON *DEUCE BIGALOW: EUROPEAN GIGOLO*

Love him, hated Hur.

—MORT SAHL ON *BEN-HUR*

Eleven years and several progressively more dreadful movies after *Signs*, director M. Night Shyamalan would be lucky to get a gig directing traffic.

—MOVIE CRITIC LOU LUMENICK ON *AFTER EARTH*

. . . An explosion in a stupid factory.
—MOVIE CRITIC LARUSHKA IVAN-ZADEH ON
A GOOD DAY TO DIE HARD

•

Stéphane Audran (Mme. Chabrol—which explains a thing or two, though not everything) combines the vacuous, far-off gaze of a blind explorer with a surly, pinched delivery of lines as if they were shoes several sizes too small.
—JOHN SIMON ON *LES BICHES*

•

Memoirs of a Geisha builds a beautiful garden, then runs an interstate through it to let more people in.
—ROB VAUX

•

Only—repeat only—for those who thought *Police Academy 5* was robbed at Oscar time.
—LEONARD MALTIN ON *POLICE ACADEMY 6*

On the IMDB trivia page it says "The most amazing thing about *Pirates 3* is that they started filming without a completed script." No, they finished filming without a completed script.
—MARK KERMODE ON *PIRATES OF THE CARIBBEAN: AT WORLD'S END*

•

Nicole "does" sexy with all the erotic charge with which one "does" the washing up. I'd rather gargle battery acid than have to watch *Birthday Girl* again.
—MOVIE CRITIC SUKHDEV SANDHU

•

No.
—LEONARD MALTIN ON *ISN'T IT ROMANTIC?*

•

Perhaps the closest Hollywood has yet come to making "Ow! My Balls!" seem like a plausible future project.
—ANDREW BARKER ON *GROWN UPS 2*

A misfire of inanities. This is a failure of epic proportions. You've got to be a genius to make a movie this bad.

—MOVIE CRITIC JOEL SIEGEL ON *THE BONFIRE OF THE VANITIES*

(Nick) Nolte looks as though he died five years ago and nobody bothered to tell him, and he runs (or staggers) with the tatty grace of the walking dead.

—MOVIE CRITIC MARC SAVLOV ON *THE GOOD THIEF*

It's marginally better than *The Cat in the Hat*, though that's like saying suffocation is mildly more amusing than drowning.

—SEAN O'CONNELL ON *GARFIELD: THE MOVIE*

When you think of the great Marguerite Moreno, who created the role, and then look at this performance, exact replicas of which have already earned Miss]Katharine] Hepburn two ill-deserved Oscars, you may wish to forsake the auditorium for the vomitorium.

—JOHN SIMON ON *THE MADWOMAN OF CHAILLOT*

Inviting her to review one of your pictures is like inviting the Boston Strangler to massage your neck.

—BILLY WILDER ON FILM CRITIC JUDITH CRIST

No matter what they're charging to get in, it's worth more to get out.

—ROGER EBERT ON *ARMAGEDDON*

Chapter

· · · · · · · · · · ·

XIII

Sic 'em-Sie Deutsch?:
Foreign Insults in Translation

Spanish:

The donkey knows more than you.

•

You are as stupid as the dog.

•

You are uglier than a monkey's butt.

•

I s**t on your bitch of a mother.

•

I hope you get f*****d by a fish.

•

You have a face like the back of a refrigerator.

•

You're so ugly you made an onion cry.

•

Why don't you suck butter from my ass?

I s**t in the milk!

French:

Go back to the whore who gave birth to you.

As a child, was your cradle rocked too close to the wall?

You've got a face that would blow off manhole covers!

Your mother sucks bears in the forest.

You are as smart as the bottom of your feet.

You smell like beef and cheese.

You are a badly groomed merino sheep.

You have the brain of a cheese sandwich.

Your mother is so small her head smells of feet.

You have the body of a dog and the IQ of a five-year-old.

You are a potato with the face of a guinea pig.

You speak French like a Spanish cow.

Italian:

Cursed be the souls of your best dead relatives.

You are as ignorant as a slap in the water.

You're not even good at dying.

You're the semen your mother should have swallowed.

Take a dump in your hand and then slap yourself.

Ah, good for nothing, feather, full of shit, bed pisser, jack of the harpsichord, shirt on the arse, loop of the hanged, hard-headed mule!

From ancient Irish:

You're as thick as a bull's walt [erection].

May they hear the curse and the malediction of the saints of Ireland!

Short life to you on this side, and hell on the other!

May the cat eat you, and may the devil eat the cat.

I will destroy the beauty of your face.

May he not complete his year!

Their lands will be boglands and thickets forever.

May it be death by spear point that takes him!

He's as thick as manure and only half as useful.

No one knows what dog birthed you out onto a dunghill.

May misfortune stick to him.

Two horse's ears on you! May you be a laughingstock!

O shit of a flapping dun-colored crane!

Hesitant speech on your successor forever!

•

May none spring from him but shoemakers and comb-makers, or people of that kind.

•

May you be beneath notice.

•

Foreign soil over you!

•

My curse and the curse of the king of heaven on all those within your house!

Chinese:

Wear a green hat [the sign of a male brothel worker].

•

Your mother is a big turtle.

•

Go pat a horse's ass.

Yiddish:

All problems I have in my heart should go to his head.

One misfortune is too few for him.

Let what I wish on him come true—most, even half, even just ten percent.

One misfortune is too few for him.

Black sorrow is all that his mother should see of him.

He should marry the daughter of the Angel of Death.

She should have stones and not children.

He should drink too much castor oil.

He should get so sick as to cough up his mother's milk.

He should give it all away to doctors.

Let him suffer and remember.

Throw salt in his eyes, pepper in his nose.

Stones on his bones.

A cramp in his body.

Leeches should drink him dry.

He should laugh with lizards.

He should go crazy and run through the streets.

They should free a madman, and lock him up.

●

He should grow a wooden tongue.

●

He should get a hernia.

●

God should visit upon him the best of the Ten Plagues.

●

Venereal disease should consume his body.

●

A young child should be named after him [naming a baby after a living person is considered bad luck].

●

I should outlive him long enough to bury him.

●

He should see everything, but have no reason to buy it.

God should bless him with three people: One should grab him, the second should stab him, and the third should hide him.

•

As many years as he's walked on his feet, let him walk on his hands, and for the rest of the time he should crawl along on his behind.

•

Ten ships of gold should be his and the money should only make him sick.

•

He should have a large store, and whatever people ask for he shouldn't have, and what he does have shouldn't be requested.

•

A hundred houses shall he have, in every house a hundred rooms and in every room twenty beds, and a delirious fever should drive him from bed to bed.

•

All his teeth should fall out except one to make him suffer.

On summer days, he should mourn, and on wintry nights, he should torture himself.

•

God should bestow him with everything his heart desires, but he should have no arms or legs, and not be able to use his tongue.

•

He should be transformed into a chandelier, to hang by day and to burn by night.

•

He should have Pharaoh's plagues sprinkled with Job's scabs.

•

He should crap blood and pus.

•

He should hang himself with a sugar rope and have a sweet death.

•

His stomach should rumble so badly, you'll think it was a Purim noisemaker.

Others:

May your fingers change into fishing hooks,

and you get an itch in your balls.

—AFRIKAANS

You are ass-dandruff!

—RUSSIAN

I can blow farts in your spoon when the soup is too hot for you.

—ROMANIAN

May God give you to search for your children with a Geiger counter.

—SERBIAN

May your house be live on CNN [that is, may your house be bombed

and then be on the news].

—SERBIAN

Sweat of a lizard's ass.

—HINDI

•

Piss into a transformer.

—FINNISH

•

Your mother married a reindeer!

—FINNISH

•

May a violin bow enter your anus.

—TURKISH

•

Try to paint my fart.

—IRANIAN

Chapter

· · · · · · · · · · ·

XIV

Way off Base: Sports Insults

Although golf was originally restricted to wealthy, overweight Protestants, today it's open to anybody who owns hideous clothing.
—DAVE BARRY

The only time he opens his mouth is to change feet.
—DAVID FEHERTY ON FELLOW GOLFER NICK FALDO

He has a face like a warthog that's been stung by a wasp.
—DAVID FEHERTY ON FELLOW GOLFER COLIN MONTGOMERIE

She's about as cuddly as a dead hedgehog. The Alsatians in her yard would go about in pairs for protection.
—JOCKEY JOHN FRANCOME ON
RACEHORSE TRAINER JENNY PITMAN

Cross-country skiing is great if you live in a small country.
—STEVEN WRIGHT

Dennis has become like a prostitute, but now it's gotten ridiculous, to the point where he will do anything humanly possible to make money.
—CHARLES BARKLEY ON BASKETBALL PLAYER DENNIS RODMAN

Basketball, a game which won't be fit for people until they set the basket umbilicus-high and return the giraffes to the zoo.
—POET OGDEN NASH

He couldn't bowl a hoop downhill.
—ENGLISH CRICKETER FRED TRUEMAN ON
CRICKETER IAN BOTHAM

A lot of people are using two-piece cues nowadays. Alex Higgins hasn't got one because they don't come with instructions.
—SNOOKER PLAYER STEVE DAVIS ON SNOOKER POOL WORLD
CHAMPION ALEX HIGGINS

Like a Volvo, Björn Borg is rugged, has good after-sales service, and is very dull.
—CLIVE JAMES ON TENNIS STAR BJÖRN BORG

Martina was so far in the closet she was in

danger of being a garment bag.

—RITA MAE BROWN ON TENNIS

CHAMPION MARTINA NAVRATILOVA

McEnroe was as charming as always, which means that he was as

charming as a dead mouse in a loaf of bread.

—CLIVE JAMES ON TENNIS STAR AND

COMMENTATOR JOHN MCENROE

I'm not having points taken off me by an incompetent old fool. You're

the pits of the world.

—JOHN MCENROE TO AN UMPIRE

You can't see as well as these f***ing flowers—and

they're f***ing plastic.

—JOHN MCENROE TO A LINE JUDGE

What other problems do you have besides being
unemployed, a moron and a dork?
—JOHN MCENROE TO A SPECTATOR

Kevin Keegan isn't fit to lace my boots—or my whiskies.
—SOCCER STAR GEORGE BEST

The bad news for Saddam Hussein is that he's just been
sentenced to the death penalty. The good news for Saddam
is that David Beckham is taking it.
—ANONYMOUS BRITISH SOCCER COMMENTATOR

Football combines the two worst features of American life: It is
violence punctuated by committee meetings.
—GEORGE WILL

If a man watches three football games in a row, he should
be declared legally dead.
—ERMA BOMBECK

Football is a game designed to keep coal miners off the streets.
—JIMMY BRESLIN

He is phony, using his blackness to get his way.
—JOE FRAZIER ON MUHAMMAD ALI

Joe Frazier is so ugly he should donate his face to the
US Bureau of Wildlife.
—MUHAMMAD ALI

[He's] so ugly, when he sweats the sweat runs backwards over his head
to avoid his face!
—MUHAMMAD ALI ON AN OPPONENT

Sometimes Howard makes me wish I was a dog, and he was a fireplug.
—MUHAMMAD ALI ON SPORTS COMMENTATOR HOWARD COSELL

You! You're the child who rhapsodizes about the infield-fly rule.

I'm sure you'll have a fine career.

—HOWARD COSELL TO SPORTSCASTER BOB COSTAS

I did not call [Boston Red Sox manager Darrell] Johnson an idiot.

Someone else did, and I just agreed.

—PITCHER JIM PALMER AT THE ALL-STAR GAME

George Steinbrenner is the center of evil in the universe.

—BEN AFFLECK ON THE FORMER NEW YORK YANKEES OWNER

One's a born liar, and the other's been convicted.

**—BILLY MARTIN ON NEW YORK YANKEE SUPERSTAR REGGIE
JACKSON AND FORMER OWNER GEORGE STEINBRENNER**

With the A's, we depended upon pitching and speed to win. With
the Giants, we depended upon pitching and power to win. With the
Indians, we depended upon an act of God.

—BASEBALL MANAGER ALVIN DARK, REVIEWING HIS CAREER

If I could hit the ball that way, I'd take off my toe plate and retire from pitching. In fact, if I hit the way you do, I think I'd also retire from baseball.

—BASEBALL PITCHER BOB GIBSON TO TEAMMATE CURT FLOOD DURING BATTING PRACTICE

Major league baseball has asked its players to stop tossing baseballs into the stands during games, because they say fans fight over them and they get hurt. In fact, the Florida Marlins said that's why they never hit any home runs. It's a safety issue.

—JAY LENO

I don't know but somebody told me they were waiters at the Last Supper.

—FORMER LOS ANGELES DODGERS MANAGER TOMMY LASORDA WHEN ASKED THE AGES OF TWO VETERAN PITCHERS

Fly fishing may be a very pleasant amusement; but angling or float fishing I can only compare to a stick and a string, with a worm at one end and a fool at the other.

—SAMUEL JOHNSON

Fishing is boring, unless you catch an actual fish, and then it is disgusting.

—DAVE BARRY

Bob Kelly was so dumb, they should have written his name on the Stanley Cup in crayon.

—PHILADELPHIA FLIERS ANNOUNCER GENE HART ON HOCKEY PLAYER BOB "HOUND DOG" KELLY

Dear UT St., Enjoy the LOSS

—BRIGHAM YOUNG UNIVERSITY SCOREBOARD OPERATOR AFTER BYU DEFEATED RIVAL UTAH STATE

What the [expletive]? Who ordered this crap?
I wouldn't feed this to my dog!
—MINNESOTA VIKINGS PLAYER RANDY MOSS
ON THE LOCKER ROOM FOOD

You take this [suit you're wearing] home and you burn it . . . So when
you get done with this . . . you should be butt-ass-naked and burn it.
And the shoes too, just burn them.
Burn it . . . Vaseline . . . kerosene . . . whatever . . . burn it.
—NBA PLAYER KEVIN GARNETT CRITICIZING
COMMENTATOR RICK SAGER'S CLOTHING

Note: The Chicago Cubs, which hadn't won a World Series since 1908
and last appeared in a Series in 1945, won the 2016 World Series.
Nevertheless, in the interest of snide humor, consider these jibes for
their historic interest . . .
It's hard to put your finger on it. You have to have a dullness of mind
and spirit to play here. I went through psychoanalysis and that helped
me deal with my Cubness.
—JIM BROSNAN, FORMER CUBS PITCHER

Noise pollution can't be that much of a problem.

There's nothing to cheer about.

—ILLINOIS STATE LEGISLATOR JOHN F. DUNN ARGUING FOR THE INSTALLATION OF LIGHTS AT WRIGLEY FIELD

If I managed the Cubs, I'd be an alcoholic.

—BASEBALL MANAGER WHITEY HERZOG

There's nothing wrong with this team that more pitching, more fielding, and more hitting couldn't help.

—MAJOR LEAGUE BASEBALL PLAYER BILL BUCKNER

The Cubs were taking batting practice, and the pitching machine threw a no-hitter.

—ANONYMOUS RADIO ANNOUNCER

Would the lady who left her nine kids at Wrigley Field
please pick them up immediately? They are beating the
Cubs 4–0 in the seventh inning.
— RADIO DEEJAY

One thing you learn as a Cubs fan: When you bought your ticket, you
could bank on seeing the bottom of the ninth.
— ANNOUNCER JOE GARAGIOLA

Q: Did you hear about the new Cubs soup?
A: Two sips and then you choke.

The latest diet is better than the Pritikin Diet: You eat only when the
Cubs win.
— PIANIST GEORGE SHEARING

Chapter

· · · · · · · · · · ·

XV

Diploma Immunity: College Insults

Q: What's the difference between the University of Alabama football team and Cheerios?

A: One belongs in a bowl. The other doesn't.

Q: Did you hear about the Auburn quarterback who tried to throw himself on the floor in a fit of rage?

A: He missed.

Q: Why do Arizona students have TGIF on their shoes?

A. Toes Go In First

Q: What do you get when you drive quickly through the Arizona State Sun Devil campus?

A: An undergraduate degree.

Q: Why do Arkansas Razorbacks put copies of their diplomas in the window of their vehicles?

A: So they can park in handicap spaces.

Q: How do you get an Auburn student off your porch?
A: Pay him for the pizza.

•

Q: What do you say when you see a Bowling Green State University grad in a suit?
A: Will the defendant please rise?

•

Q: What does the average California State University student get on his SAT?
A: Drool.

•

Q: What should you do if you find three University of Connecticut football fans buried up to their necks in cement?
A: Get more cement.

•

Q: Do you know why the Duke University football team should change its name to the "Opossums"?
A: Because they play dead at home and get killed on the road.

Q: What do you get when you cross a Georgia Bulldog and a pig?

A: Nothing. There's some things that a pig will not do.

•

Q: How many Kentucky Wildcats does it take to change a lightbulb?

A: None. Lava lamps don't burn out.

•

Q: Did you hear about the fire in Louisiana State University's football dorm that destroyed 20 books?

A: Yes, but the real tragedy was that fifteen hadn't been colored yet.

•

Q: Did you hear about the power outage at the University of Minnesota library?

A: Forty students were stuck on the escalator for three hours.

•

Q: How do you make University of Notre Dame cookies?

A: Put them in a big Bowl and beat for three hours.

Q: How many Ohio State Buckeyes does it take to change a lightbulb?

A: Two—one to change the light bulb and one to crack under the pressure.

Q: What do Ohio State and pot have in common?

A: They both get smoked in bowls.

Q: What do you get when you breed a groundhog and Purdue University?

A: Six more weeks of bad football.

Q: How many University of Tennessee freshmen does it take to change a light bulb?

A: None. It's a sophomore course.

Q: What do they call students who go to Harvard?

A: Yale rejects.

Chapter

. . . .

XVI

Maternal In-stinks!: Yo' Mamas

Yo' mama is so dumb that she got fired from the M&M factory for throwing away all the Ws.

●

Yo' mama is so dumb when her sergeant in the Army yelled, "Enemy at three o'clock!", she asked, "What do I do until then?"

●

Yo' mama is so dumb when she hears it's chilly outside, she gets a bowl and a spoon.

●

Yo' mama' is so dumb that it took her two hours to watch "60 Minutes."

●

Yo' mama is so dumb she tried to climb Mountain Dew.

●

Yo' mama is so dumb she thinks Fleetwood Mac is a new hamburger at McDonalds'.

Yo' mama is so dumb she bought tickets to Xbox Live.

Yo' mama is so dumb she stood on a chair to raise her IQ.

Yo' mama is so dumb she thinks menopause is a button on a VCR.

Yo' mama is so dumb she goes to the Apple Store to get a
Big Mac burger.

Yo' mama is so stupid she sold her car for gas money.

Yo' mama is so stupid she waited for a "stop" sign to turn to "go."

Yo' mama is so dumb she cut open a pineapple and asked, "SpongeBob,
where are you?"

Yo' mama is so dumb, she thought Spotify was a stain remover!

Yo' mama is so dumb when the judge said, "Order!", she said "A burger and a malted, please."

•

Yo' mama is so dumb she put a battery in water to make an energy drink.

•

Yo' mama is so dumb she put two pieces of candy in her ears and thought she was listening to Eminem.

•

Yo' mama is so dumb she took her dog to Pet Smart for an IQ test.

•

Yo' mama is so dumb she went to the dentist to get her Bluetooth fixed.

•

Yo' mama is so dumb, she thinks *gluteus maximus* is a Roman emperor.

Yo' mama is so dumb she looked in the mirror and said,
"You lookin' at me?"

●

Yo' mama is so dumb that when she saw the "Under 17 Not Admitted"
sign at a movie theatre, she went home and got sixteen friends.

●

Yo' mama is so stupid that when she went for a blood test, she asked for
time to study.

●

Yo' mama is so dumb she thought Dunkin' Donuts
is a basketball contest.

●

Yo' mama is so dumb that when I said, "Check out this cool new
website," she got a broom and looked for the spider.

●

Yo' mama is so dumb that she thought Boyz II Men was
a day care center.

Yo' mama is so dumb she took an umbrella to see *Purple Rain*.

•

Yo' mama is so dumb that under "Education" on her job application, she listed "Hooked on Phonics."

•

Yo' mama is so dumb she watches *The Three Stooges* and takes notes.

•

Yo' mama is so stupid that when I asked her to play a game of "one-on-one basketball" with me, she said, "OK, but who's on my team?"

Chapter

· · · · · · · · · · ·

XVII

Editor's Choice:
Selected Goodies and Baddies

New York City lawyer Joseph Choate once opposed a lawyer at a court in Westchester County, north of the city. In an effort to mock him, local lawyer cautioned the jury not to be taken in by Choate's "Chesterfieldian urbanity."

In rebuttal, Choate urged the jury not to be taken in by the other lawyer's "Westchesterfieldian suburbanity."

•

While traveling by train, *New York Tribune* publisher Horace Greeley noticed a fellow passenger reading the rival *Sun* and asked why he did not read the *Tribune*.

"I take the *Tribune* too," the man replied. "I use it to wipe my arse with."

"Keep it up," Greeley declared, "and eventually you'll have more brains in your arse than you have in your head."

•

George S. Kaufman said to Marc Connolly, "I like your bald head, Marc. It feels just like my wife's behind."

Connolly replied, rubbing his pate, "So it does, George!"

At a dinner party thrown by the producer Arthur Hornblow and his wife, the elderly Mrs. Hornblow never stopped talking about her brief theatrical career.

When she said for the umpteenth time "Well, when I was on the stage . . .," Dorothy Parker turned to her dinner companion and said in a loud whisper: "Nonsense, in those days, boys played all the women's parts!"

●

Clare Booth Luce gestured to Dorothy Parker to precede her through the door, saying, "Age before beauty."

Parker swept on with a curt "Pearls before swine."

●

"I suppose life can never get entirely dull to an American, because whenever he can't strike up any other way to put in his time he can always get away with a few years trying to find out who his grandfather was," said a Frenchman to Mark Twain.

To which Twain replied, "Right, your excellency. But I reckon a Frenchman's got his little stand-by for a dull time, too; because when all other interests fail he can turn in and see if he can't find out who his father was."

A political rally heckler to presidential candidate Al Smith: "Go ahead Al. Tell 'em all you know. It won't take long."
Smith replied, "I'll tell 'em all we *both* know. It won't take any longer."

•

"Yes, I am a Jew, and when the ancestors of the right honorable gentleman were brutal savages in an unknown island, mine were priests in the temple of Solomon."
—Benjamin Disraeli, responding to Member of Parliament Daniel O'Connell's disparaging of Disraeli's Jewish ancestry.

•

The violinist Jacques Thibault was handed an autograph book after a concert. "There's not much room on this page," he told his fan. "What shall I write?"
Another violinist standing nearby suggested, "Write your repertoire."

When Mark Twain finished giving one of his customary after-dinner speeches, a prominent lawyer stood up, shoved his hands in his pockets, and said, "Doesn't it strike this company as unusual that a professional humorist should be so funny?"

Twain replied, "Doesn't it strike this company as unusual that a lawyer should have both hands in his own pockets?"

•

An actress told Ilka Chase, "I enjoyed reading your book. Who wrote it for you?"

Case snapped back, "Darling, I'm so glad that you liked it. Who read it to you?"

•

A singer told Miriam Hopkins: "You know, my dear, I insured my voice for fifty-thousand dollars."

Replied Hopkins: "That's wonderful. And what did you do with the money?"

•

Oscar Wilde took a curtain call at one of his plays and harangued the audience for their insensitivity to art. "You are Philistines who have invaded this sacred sanctum," he told them.

"And," shouted a voice from the audience, "you are driving us forth with the jawbone of an ass."

◉

Oscar Wilde replied to a witty remark: "I wish I had said that." The painter James McNeill Whistler, standing nearby, told him: "You will, Oscar; you will."

◉

At a party one evening, the painter James McNeill Whistler found himself cornered by a notorious bore. "You know, Mr. Whistler," the bore said, "I passed your house last night."
"Thank you," Whistler replied.

◉

Noel Coward was informed that a certain dim-witted theater manager had shot himself in the head.
Coward replied, "He must have been a marvelously good shot."

◉

Noel Coward told the American writer Edna Ferber, who was wearing a tailored suit: "You look almost like a man."
Replied Ferber: "So do you."

When the heavyset G. K. Chesterton said, "I see there has been a famine in the land," the thin George Bernard Shaw answered, "And I see the cause of it. If I were as fat as you, I would hang myself." Chesterton replied, "If I were to hang myself, I would use you for the rope."

●

George Bernard Shaw sent Sir Winston Churchill two tickets for the first night of one of his plays with a note saying: "Bring a friend—if you have one."

Churchill returned the tickets, saying he would not be able to attend but would be grateful for tickets for the second night—"if there is one."

●

An elderly dowager told a young Winston Churchill, "There are two things I don't like about you, Mr. Churchill—your politics and your mustache."

Churchill replied, "My dear madam, pray do not disturb yourself. You are not likely to come into contact with either."

Toward the end of Sir Winston Churchill's life, a member of Parliament remarked when he saw Churchill visiting the House of Commons: "They say he's potty."

Churchill overheard and replied: "They say he can't hear either."

•

Society grande dame to Winston Churchill: Winston, you're drunk.

Churchill: And you, madam, are ugly. But I shall be sober in the morning.

•

Lady Astor to Winston Churchill: Mr. Churchill, if you were my husband, I'd put poison in your tea.

Churchill: Madam, if you were my wife . . . I'd drink it.

•

After dinner one evening, a hostess entertained the house guests by playing the piano. At one point she turned to a visitor and said, "I understand you love music."

"Yes," murmured the guest politely. "But never you mind. Keep right on playing."

An actor in one of the Gilbert and Sullivan operettas told librettist William S. Gilbert, "See here, sir, I will not be bullied—I know my lines."
To which Gilbert replied, "Possibly, but you don't know mine."

●

Henry Clay, senator from Kentucky, was sitting on the porch of a Washington, DC, hotel with Daniel Webster, senator from Massachusetts. As a man leading a small herd of mules walked by, Webster commented, "Clay, there go a number of your Kentucky constituents."
Clay replied: "They must be going up to Massachusetts to teach school."

●

Congressman Joseph Reed, after Senator Henry Clay announced, "I would rather be right than be president," commented: "He doesn't have to worry. He'll never be either."

●

John Randolph, meeting political rival Henry Clay on a narrow sidewalk: "I, sir, do not step aside for a scoundrel."
Clay replied as he yielded the way, "I, on the other hand, always do."

British playwright Samuel Foote once asked a man why he continuously sang a particular song. "Because it haunts me," the man explained.

"No wonder," Foote replied, "since you are forever murdering it!"

•

Invited to attend an orgy in Paris, Voltaire accepted with pleasure. The next day, after reporting to his friends that he had enjoyed the experience, he was invited to attend again that evening.

"Ah no, my good friends," he declined, "once a philosopher, twice a pervert."

•

Right before a Christmas vacation, William Lyons Phelps, professor of literature at Yale University, marked an examination paper on which was written, "God only knows the answer to this question. Merry Christmas."

Phelps returned the exam with: "God gets an A. You get an F. Happy New Year."

•

A young actress invited by actress Ethel Barrymore to dinner not only failed to appear, but neglected to apologize or account for her absence.

A few days later, the two women unexpectedly met. "I think I was invited to your house to dinner last Thursday night," the young woman began.

"Oh, yes?" Barrymore replied. "Did you come?"

●

One evening comedian George Jessel arrived at the exclusive Stork Club with the black singer and actress Lena Horne on his arm. Sherman Billingsley, the club's owner, and his headwaiters, while hardly ardent supporters of racial equality, nevertheless treated Jessel, a regular customer, with minimal respect. The headwaiter looked through his reservation book and pretended there were no openings.

"Mr. Jessel," he finally said, "who made the reservation?"

Jessel replied, "Abraham Lincoln."

●

Arriving at church one Sunday, Henry Ward Beecher found in his mailbox a letter that contained the single word: "Fool."

During the service that morning, he related the incident to his congregation: "I have known many an instance of a man writing a letter and forgetting to sign his name, but this is the only instance I have ever known of a man signing his name and forgetting to write the letter."

When British Labour Party figure Herbert Morrison remarked that he was his own worst enemy, his rival Ernest Bevin immediately replied, "Not while I'm alive, he ain't."

•

The drama critic James Agate once approached actress Lilian Braithwaite with, "My dear lady, may I tell you something I have wanted to tell you for years: that you are the second most beautiful woman in the United Kingdom."
Braithwaite replied, "Thank you, I shall always cherish that as coming from the second-best drama critic."

•

A Harvard man and a Yale man finished at adjoining urinals. The Harvard man proceeded to the sink to wash his hands, while the Yale man went directly to the bathroom door. The Harvard man said, "At Harvard they teach us to wash our hands after we urinate."
The Yale man replied, "At Yale they teach us not to piss on our hands."

While delivering a campaign speech one day, Theodore Roosevelt was interrupted by a heckler. "I'm a Democrat!" the man shouted.

"May I ask the gentleman," Roosevelt replied, quieting the crowd, "why he is a Democrat?"

"My grandfather was a Democrat," the man replied, "My father was a Democrat and I am a Democrat."

"My friend," Roosevelt interjected, "suppose your grandfather had been a jackass and your father was a jackass. What would you then be?"

The heckler replied, "A Republican!"

•

Calvin Coolidge, who was widely known as taciturn (he was called "Silent Cal"), was approached by a woman who told him, "Mr. President, I bet my friend that I could get you to say three words to me."

Coolidge replied, "You lose."

When Calvin Coolidge and his wife were touring a chicken farm, the
foreman noted the sexual prowess of his prize rooster. "Did you know,"
he said, "that a rooster can provide his services all day
without stopping?"

"Ah," said Mrs. Coolidge. "You must tell that to my husband."

Coolidge asked the foreman. "And with the same partner?"

"Oh no," said the foreman, "always with different chickens."

Coolidge replied, "You must tell that to my wife."

The Polish pianist Ignace Paderewski was approached in Boston by
a bootblack who asked whether he wanted a shoe shine. Paderewski
looked down at the boy's dirty face. "No, but if you will wash your face,
I will give you a quarter," he said.

The boy ran to a nearby fountain and cleaned himself up, whereupon
Paderewski offered him a quarter.

The boy briefly admired it, and then returned it. "Keep it, mister," he
said, "and get yourself a haircut."

A drunk stumbled up to Groucho Marx, slapped him on the back, and
said, "You old son-of-a-gun, you probably don't remember me . . ."
"I never forget a face," Marx replied, "but in your case, I'll be glad to
make an exception."

●

Pompous young man: "I can't bear fools."
Dorothy Parker: "Apparently, your mother could."

●

"No, sir, I do not. But I shall make inquiries and inform you directly."
—A waiter to a patron who was annoyed by slow service and had asked
in annoyance, "Do you know who I am?"

●

Nazi official Hermann Goering collided with an Italian nobleman on
a crowded train platform in Rome. When the Italian demanded an
apology, Goering snapped, "I am Hermann Goering."
"As an excuse that is not enough," the nobleman replied, "but as an
explanation it is ample."

Ulysses S. Grant once entered an inn on a stormy winter's night. A number of lawyers in town for a court session were clustered around the fire. One looked up and said, "Here's a stranger, gentlemen, and by the looks of him he's traveled through hell itself to get here."

"That's right," Grant admitted.

"And how did you find things down there?" he was asked.

"Just like here," replied Grant, "the lawyers were all closest to the fire."

•

John Wilkes was an eighteenth-century English politician of radical leanings. The Earl of Sandwich, a staunch conservative with opposing views, became so irate at something Wilkes said that he exploded, "Egad sir, I do not know whether you will die on the gallows or of the pox."

To which John Wilkes replied, "That will depend, my Lord, on whether I embrace your principles or your mistress."

SELECTED QUOTED SOURCES
AND PEOPLE MENTIONED IN QUOTES

• • • • • • • • • • • • • • • • • •

Adams, Douglas (1952–2001), British writer
Adams, Joey (1911–1999), American comedian
Adams, John (1735–1826), second US president
Adams, John Quincy (1767–1848), sixth US president
Affleck, Ben (b. 1972), American actor
Aguilera, Christina (b. 1980), American pop singer
Ali, Muhammad, born Cassius Clay (1942–2016), American prizefighter
Allen, Fred (1894–1956), American radio personality and actor
Allen, Lily (b. 1985), British singer and television personality
Allen, Maryon (b. 1925), American journalist and politician
Allen, Woody (b. 1935), American comedian, actor, and film producer
Aristophanes (c. 448–388 BC), Athenian playwright
Asquith, Margot (1864–1945), British politician and writer
Astaire, Fred (1899–1987), American dancer and actor
Astor, Lady Nancy (1879–1964), British politician
Atkinson, Brooks (1894–1984), American theater critic
Auden, W. H. (1907–1973), Anglo-American poet
Austen, Jane (1775–1817), English novelist
Balzac, Honoré de (1799–1850), French writer
Bankhead, Tallulah (1902–1968), American actress
Banks, Tony (1942–2006), British Labour Party politician and cabinet minister
Baring, Maurice (1874–1945), British diplomat, journalist, and author
Barkley, Charles (b. 1963), American basketball player
Barrie, Sir James Matthew (1860–1937), British writer
Barry, Dave (b. 1947), American humor columnist
Baudelaire, Charles (1821–1867), French poet and critic
Beaton, Cecil (1904–1980), British fashion designer

Beecham, Sir Thomas (1879–1961), British orchestral conductor
Beethoven, Ludwig van (1770–1827), German composer
Begley Jr., Ed (b. 1949), American actor
Behan, Brendan (1923–1964), Irish dramatist
Bellow, Saul (1915–2005), Canadian-American author and critic
Berlioz, Hector (1803–1869), French composer
Bernhardt, Sarah (1844–1923), French actress
Bevan, Aneurin (or Ernest) (1881–1951), British statesman
Billings, Josh (1818–1885), American humorous essayist
Birkenhead, F. E. Smith, first Earl of (1872–1930), British politician
Blackwell, Richard, "Mr. Blackwell" (1922–2008), American fashion critic
Bombeck, Erma (1927–1996), author and columnist
Bonaparte, Napoleon (1769–1821), French emperor and general
Borg, Björn (b. 1956), Swedish tennis player
Boswell, James (1740–1795), Scottish author and biographer of Samuel Johnson
Boy George, stage name of George O. Dowd (b. 1961), British pop singer
Brahms, Johannes (1833–1897), German composer
Braithwaite, Lilian (1873–1948), British actress
Brann, William Cowper (1855–1898), American journalist
Breslin, Jimmy (b. 1930), American journalist
Brown, Rita Mae (b. 1944), American author and social activist
Brummel, George Bryan "Beau" (1778–1840), British dandy and wit
Bryan, William Jennings (1860–1925), American lawyer and politician
Bryson, Bill (b. 1951), American writer
Buchanan, James (1791–1868), fifteenth US president
Bush, George H. W. (b. 1924), forty-first US president
Bush, George W. (b. 1946), forty-third US president
Butler, Samuel (1835–1902), British novelist and critic
Byron, George Gordon Noel, sixth Baron Byron (1788–1824), British romantic poet
Campbell, Mrs. Patrick (1865–1940), English actress
Capone, Alphonse "Al" (1899–1947), American gangster
Capote, Truman (1924–1984), American author
Carlyle, Thomas (1795–1881), British historian

Carter, Jimmy (b. 1924), thirty-ninth US president
Cassavetes, John (1929–1989), American actor
Cave, Nick (b. 1957), Australian rock singer
Chandler, Raymond (1888–1959), American author
Chase, Ilka (1905–1978), American actress and writer
Chesterton, G. K. (1874–1936), British author
Choate, Joseph (1932–1967), American lawyer and diplomat
Chopin, Frederic (1810–1849), Polish composer
Christgau, Robert (b. 1942), American music critic
Churchill, Sir Winston (1874–1965), British statesman and author
Clapton, Eric (b. 1945), English rock and blues musician
Clay, Henry (1777–1852), American politician
Clemenceau, Georges (1841–1929), French statesman
Clemens, Samuel: see Mark Twain
Clinton, Hillary (b. 1947), US senator and cabinet official
Clinton, William Jefferson "Bill" (b. 1946), forty-second US president
Cobb, Irvin S. (1876–1944), American humor author and newspaper columnist
Coleridge, Samuel Taylor (1772–1834), British romantic poet
Compton-Burnett, Dame Ivy (1884–1969), English novelist
Conrad, Joseph (1857–1924), British novelist
Constable, John (1776–1837), English painter
Coolidge, Calvin (1872–1933), thirtieth US president
Copland, Aaron (1900–1990), American composer
Corbett, Leonora (1908-1960), British stage actress
Cosell, Howard (1918–1995), American sports broadcaster
Costello, Elvis, stage name of Declan Patrick MacManus (b. 1954), British rock musician
Coward, Noel (1899–1973), British playwright and composer
Crawford, Joan (1908–1977), American movie star
Cripps, Sir (Richard) Stafford (1889–1952), British politician
Crockett, Davy (1786–1836), American frontiersman
cummings, e. e. (1894–1962), American author
Dangerfield, Rodney (1921–2004), American comedian
Dassin, Jules (1911–2008), American film director

Davies, Robertson (1913–1995), Canadian novelist

Davis, Bette (1908–1989), American film actress

Davis, Jefferson (1808–1898), president of the Confederacy during the Civil War

Dewey, Thomas E. (1902–1971), American politician, including presidential candidate

Dickens, Charles (1812–1870), British novelist

Disraeli, Benjamin, first Earl of Beaconsfield (1804–1881), British statesman and author

Dole, Robert "Bob" (b. 1923), US politician

Dykstra, Lillian (1894–1977), American educator and writer

Ebert, Roger (1943–2013), American movie reviewer

Eisenhower, Dwight David (1890–1969), thirty-fourth US president

Eliot, George (1819–1880), pseudonym of Mary Ann Evans, British novelist

Eliot, T. S. (1888–1965), British poet and winner of the Nobel Prize for Literature

Emerson, Ralph Waldo (1803–1882), American philosopher and poet

Fadiman, Clifton (1904–1999), literary critic

Faulkner, William (1897–1962), American author and Nobel Prize winner

Fields, W. C. (1880–1946), American comic actor

Fitzgerald, F. Scott (1896–1940), American novelist

Flaubert, Gustave (1821–1880), French novelist

Foote, Samuel (1720–1777), British playwright

Ford, Gerald R. (1913–2006), 38th U.S. president

Fowler, Gene (1890–1960), American journalist

Frazier, Joe (1944–2011), American heavyweight boxing champion

Freud, Sigmund (1856–1939), Austrian psychoanalyst

Frost, Sir David (1939–2013), British television personality

Frost, Robert (1874–1963), American poet

Gardner, Ava (1922–1990), American actress

Geithner, Timothy (b. 1961), American financier and cabinet official

George, David Lloyd (1863–1945), UK prime minister

Glasgow, Ellen (1873–1945), American author

Goldwater, Barry (1909–1998), US senator

Grant, Ulysses S. (1822–1885), eighteenth US president

Greeley, Horace (1811–1872), American newspaper editor

Grohl, David (b. 1969), American rock musician

Hamilton, Alexander (1757–1804), American statesman
Hardie, James Keir (1856–1915), British politician
Harriman, W. Averill (1891–1986), American politician and diplomat
Hart, Moss (1904–1961), American playwright and theater director
Hawthorne, Nathaniel (1804–1864), American writer
Hellman, Lillian (1905–1984), American dramatist
Hemingway, Ernest (1899–1961), American writer
Henry, O., pseudonym of William Sydney Porter (1862–1910), American short-story writer
Hepburn, Katharine (1907–2003), American actress
Hoffman, Abbie (1936–1989), American political activist
Hoover, Herbert (1874–1964), thirty-first US president
Hopkins, Miriam (1902–1972), American actress
Hopper, Hedda (1885–1966), American actress and gossip columnist
Houston, Sam (1793–1863), American politician and soldier
Hunt, Leigh (1784–1859), English essayist and poet
Huston, John (1906–1987), American film actor and director
Huxley, Aldous (1894–1963), British novelist
Ickes, Harold (1874–1952), American politician
Irving, Washington (1783–1859), American author and diplomat
Ivins, Molly (b. 1944), American journalist
Jackson, Andrew (1767–1845), seventh US president
Jackson, Jesse (b. 1941), American civil rights leader and politician
Jagger, Mick (b. 1943), British lead singer of The Rolling Stones
James, Clive (b. 1939), Australian critic and television personality
James, Henry (1843–1916), American novelist and critic
James, William (1842–1910), American philosopher
Jefferson, Thomas (1743–1826), third US president
Jobs, Steve (1955–2011), American inventor and entrepreneur
Johnson, Andrew (1808–1875), seventeenth US president
Johnson, Boris (b. 1964), British politician and journalist
Johnson, Lyndon B. (1908–1973), thirty-sixth US president
Johnson, Samuel (1709–1784), English author
Jonson, Ben (1572–1637), English dramatist and poet

Joyce, James (1882–1941), Irish novelist
Kaufman, George S. (1889–1961), American playwright, director, and journalist
Keating, Paul (b. 1944), Australian politician
Kennedy, John Fitzgerald (1917–1963), thirty-fifth US president
Kerouac, Jack (1922–1969), American Beat Generation novelist
Kerr, Walter (1913–1996), American theater critic
Kinnock, Neil (b. 1942), British politician
Kipling, Rudyard (1865–1936), British poet and author
Kramer, Leonie (1924–2016), Australian academician and author
Lady Gaga, stage name of Stefani Germanotta (b. 1986), American pop singer
Lamb, Charles (1775–1834), English essayist
Landor, Walter Savage (1775–1864), British poet
Lawrence, D. H. (1885–1930), British novelist
Leno, Jay (b. 1950), American comedian and TV host
Leonard, Hugh, pseudonym of John Keyes Byrne (1926–2009), Irish playwright and author
Levant, Oscar (1906–1972), American pianist and wit
Lewis, C. S. (1898–1963), British writer
Lincoln, Abraham (1809–1865), sixteenth US president
Linklater, Eric (1899–1974), Scottish author
Lloyd George, David (1863–1945), British statesman
Longworth, Alice Roosevelt (1884–1980), American political hostess
Love, Courtney (b. 1964), American pop musician
Lowell, James Russell (1819–1891), American editor and diplomat
Luce, Clare Booth (1903–1987), American editor, playwright, and diplomat
Macaulay, Thomas Babington, first Baron Macaulay (1800–1859), British historian, writer, and
    politician
Macdonald, Dwight (1906–1982), American author and editor
Madonna stage name of Madonna Louise Ciccone (b. 1968), American pop singer
Mailer, Norman (1923–2007), American novelist and essayist
Maltin, Leonard (b. 1950), movie reviewer
Martial, born Marcus Valerius Martialis (AD 40–104), Roman poet
Martin, Billy (1928–1989), former New York Yankees manager
Marvell, Andrew (1621–1678), British metaphysical poet

Masefield, John (1876–1967), British poet
Matthau, Walter (1920–2000), American actor
Maurois, Andre (1885–1967), French author
McAdoo, William (1863–1941), American lawyer and politician
McCarthy, Mary (1912–1989), American writer
McClellan, General George (1826–1885), American Civil War general
McEnroe, John (b. 1959), American tennis player
Mencken, Henry Louis (1880–1956), American editor and critic
Mercury, Freddie (1946–1991), Zanzibar musician and singer
Midler, Bette (b. 1945), American actress
Miller, Henry (1891–1980), American author
Milton, John (1608–1674), British poet
Mitchell, Joni (b. 1943), Canadian singer-songwriter
Mitford, Nancy (1904–1973), English writer
Mizner, Wilson (1876–1933), American playwright
Moore, George (1852–1933), English author
Nathan, George Jean (1882–1958), American editor and drama critic
Nicolson, Harold (1886–1968), British politician
Nietzsche, Friedrich Wilhelm (1844–1900), German philosopher
Obama, Barack (b. 1961), forty-fourth US president
O'Neill, Eugene (1888–1953), American dramatist and Nobel Prize winner
O'Rourke, P. J. (b. 1947), American political satirist
Paar, Jack (1918–2004), American humorist and television personality
Paine, Thomas (1737–1809), British-American political activist
Palmer, Jim (b. 1945), American baseball player
Parker, Dorothy (1893–1967), American writer and critic
Parton, Dolly (b. 1946), American country singer and businesswoman
Pegler, Westbrook (1894–1969), American newspaper columnist
Perelman, S. J. (1904–1979), American humorist and author
Phelps, William Lyon (1865–1943), US educator and literary critic
Pompadour, Madame de, (1721–1764), French courtesan
Pope, Alexander (1688–1744), British poet and satirist
Pound, Ezra (1885–1972), American poet

Prince, born Prince Rogers Nelson (1958–2016), American singer and musician

Rabelais, François (c.1490–1553), French writer and physician

Ratoff, Gregory (1897–1960), Russian-American film actor and director

Reade, W. W. (1838–1875), British historian and explorer

Reagan, Ronald (1911–2004), fortieth US president

Richards, Ann (1933–2006), American politician and journalist

Richards, I. A. (1893–1979), English literary critic

Richards, Keith (b. 1943), British musician and songwriter

Rinehart, Mary Roberts (1876–1958), American novelist

Rivers, Joan (1933–2014), American comedian

Rock, Chris (b. 1965), American comedian and actor

Rogers, Will (1879–1935), American humorist

Roosevelt, Franklin Delano (1882–1945), thirty-second US president

Roosevelt, Theodore (1858–1919), twenty-sixth US president

Rostand, Edmond (1868–1918), French poet and dramatist

Roth, David Lee (b. 1954), American rock musician

Rushton, Willie (1937–1996), British satirist and artist

Ruskin, John (1819–1900), British art critic

Russell, Bertrand (1872–1970), British philosopher and mathematician

Sahl, Mort (b. 1927), American humorist and political commentator

Saint-Saens, Charles-Camille (1835–1921), French composer

Sand, George, pseudonym of Amandine Dupin (1804–1876), French novelist

Sandburg, Carl (1878–1967), American biographer and poet

Schwarzenegger, Arnold (b. 1947), Austrian-American actor and politician

Scott, George C. (1927–1999), American film actor

Scott, Sir Walter (1771–1832), Scottish novelist and poet

Shakespeare, William (1564–1616), British dramatist

Shales, Tom (b. 1944), American television critic

Shaw, George Bernard (1856–1950), Irish dramatist and critic

Shaw, Henry Wheeler, see Billings, Josh

Sheed, Wilfred (1930–2011), British-American author and critic

Shelley, Percy Bysshe (1792–1822), English poet

Shelton, Blake (b. 1976), American country musician

Sheridan , Richard Brinsley (1751–1816), British playwright and politician

Simon, John (b. 1925), American theater, film, and book critic

Siskel, Gene (1946–1999), American movie reviewer

Sitwell, Dame Edith (1887–1964), English poet and critic

Skelton, Red (1913–1997), American comedian

Smith, Goldwin (1823–1910), British historian and journalist

Smith, Sydney (1771–1845), British author and cleric

Stein, Gertrude (1874–1946), American experimental writer

Stevenson, Robert Louis (1850–1894), British novelist

Stone, I. F. (1907–1989), American journalist

Stone, Irving (1903–1989), American author

Stone, Sharon (b. 1958), American actress

Streisand, Barbra (b. 1942), American singer and actress

Strong, George Templeton (1820–1875), American composer

Swift, Jonathan (1667–1745), British writer and satirist

Taft, William Howard (1857–1930), twenty-seventh US president

Talleyrand-Perigord, Charles-Maurice de (1754–1838), French statesman

Taylor, Elizabeth (1928–2011), Anglo-American actress

Tchaikovsky, Pyotr Ilyich (1840–1893), Russian composer

Tennyson, Alfred (1809–1892), British poet

Thatcher, Margaret (1925–2013), British prime minister

Theroux, Paul (b. 1941), American travel author and journalist

Thomas, Dylan (1914–1953), Welsh poet

Thompson, Hunter S. (1939–2005), American writer

Thoreau, Henry David (1817–1862), American writer and philosopher

Thurber, James (1894–1961), American humorist

Toscanini, Arturo (1867–1957), Italian-American orchestral conductor

Toynbee, Arnold (1852–1883), English economic historian, philosopher, and reformer

Trollope, Anthony (1815–1882), British novelist

Trudeau, Pierre (1919–2000), Canadian prime minister

Truman, Harry S. (1884–1972), thirty-third US president

Trump, Donald J. (b. 1946), businessman and forty-fifth US president

Twain, Mark, pen name of Samuel L. Clemens (1835–1910), American humorist and author

Vidal, Gore (1929–2012), American writer

Voltaire, pen name of François-Marie de Arouet (1694–1778), French philosopher and author

Wagner, Richard (1813–1883), German composer

Waits, Tom (b. 1949), American musician and songwriter

Walpole, Horace (1717–1797), British author

Warhol, Andy (1928–1987), American pop artist

Washington, George (1732–1799), first US president

Waugh, Evelyn (1903–1966), English writer

Webster, Daniel (1782–1852), American congressman

Wells, H. G. (1866–1946), British author

Wesley, John (1703–1791), British religious leader

Whistler, James Abbott McNeill (1834–1903), American artist

Whitman, Walt (1819–1892), American poet

Wilde, Oscar (1854–1900), Irish dramatist

Wilder, Billy (1906–2002), Austrian-American film director

Wilhelm II (1859–1941), German emperor

Will, George F. (b. 1941), American political journalist

Williams, Robin (1951–2014), American actor and comedian

Wilson, Edmund (1895–1972), American critic and author

Wilson, Woodrow (1856–1924), twenty-eighth US president

Wodehouse, P. G. (1881–1975), English-American novelist

Woolf, Virginia (1882–1941), English novelist and essayist

Woollcott, Alexander (1887–1943), American drama critic and journalist

Wright, Steven (b. 1955), American comedian

Yeats, William Butler (1865–1939), Irish poet

Youngman, Henny (1906–1998), American comedian

Zangwell, Israel (1864–1926), British author